Beyond Illusion

Also by David R. Hawkins, M.D., Ph.D.

BOOKS

*Book of Slides: The Complete Collection Presented at the 2002–2011
Lectures with Clarifications*

Discovery of the Presence of God: Devotional Nonduality

The Ego Is Not the Real You: Wisdom to Transcend the Mind and Realize the Self

*The Evolution of Consciousness: Navigating the Levels of Awareness
and Unlocking Spiritual Potential*

The Eye of the I: From Which Nothing Is Hidden

Healing and Recovery

I: Reality and Subjectivity

*In the World, But Not of It: Transforming Everyday
Experience into a Spiritual Path*

The Highest Level of Enlightenment

Letting Go: The Pathway of Surrender

*The Map of Consciousness Explained: A Proven Energy
Scale to Actualize Your Ultimate Potential*

Power vs. Force: The Hidden Determinants of Human Behavior

Reality, Spirituality and Modern Man

*Success Is for You: Using Heart-Centered Power Principles for
Lasting Abundance and Fulfillment*

*Transcending the Levels of Consciousness:
The Stairway to Enlightenment*

Truth vs. Falsehood: How to Tell the Difference

*The Wisdom of Dr. David R. Hawkins: Classic Teachings on the
Spiritual Truth and Enlightenment*

Audio Programs

How to Surrender to God

Live Life as a Prayer

The Map of Consciousness Explained

All of the above are available at your local bookstore, or may be ordered by visiting:

Hay House USA: www.hayhouse.com®
Hay House Australia: www.hayhouse.com.au
Hay House UK: www.hayhouse.co.uk
Hay House India: www.hayhouse.co.in

Beyond Illusion

Exploring Perception, Ego,
and Meditation on the Path to Truth

David R. Hawkins, M.D., Ph.D.

HAY HOUSE LLC
Carlsbad, California • New York City
London • Sydney • New Delhi

Published in the United States by:
Hay House LLC, www.hayhouse.com®
P.O. Box 5100, Carlsbad, CA, 92018-5100

Cover design: Julie Davison
Interior design: Stefan Killen, Red+Company

The original talk titles for this lecture series, The Way to God, are *Perception and Illusion: Distortions of Reality* and *Realizing the Root of Consciousness: Meditative and Contemplative Techniques*.

Cataloging-in-Publication Data is on file at the Library of Congress.

Tradepaper ISBN: 978-1-4019-7710-8
E-book ISBN: 978-1-4019-7711-5

10 9 8 7 6 5 4 3 2 1
1st edition, April 2025

Printed in the United States of America

This product uses responsibly sourced papers, including recycled materials and materials from other controlled sources.

The authorized representative in the EU for product safety and compliance is Penguin Random House Ireland, Morrison Chambers, 32 Nassau Street, Dublin D02 YH68, Ireland. https://eu-contact.penguin.ie

CONTENTS

INTRODUCTION

When Dr. Hawkins presented his 2002 lecture series, his aim was to share the newly realized and life-changing information that was revealed to him from his own subjective experience and research. Because of his love for humanity, his teachings help to relieve the suffering and stress we all experience and bring clarity for those interested in spiritual progress and advanced levels of consciousness, which includes the highest states of enlightenment a person can reach.

Dr. Hawkins also wanted to dispel the untruths—those beliefs and perceptions that humankind trusts to be right and true, but in reality, are blocks to real freedom, higher awareness, and spiritual realization.

How did he accomplish this? Dr. Hawkins discovered that he could use the muscle testing method within consciousness itself. He used this method to calibrate the truth or not-truth about anything. Excitedly, he also saw that mankind now has a compass that would be the beacon of light that clears the cobwebs, and aligns the spiritual pathway to a more direct, positive, and gratifying life journey.

One major area that Dr. Hawkins specifically focuses on, is to describe the structure of the ego and how it *can* be transcended. He says:

> . . , if we understand something about the functions of the
> ego, its mechanisms, and its structure, and we observe its

functioning in the world, it's an easy step then to see that it's probably going on within myself. If it's not going on within myself, I wouldn't find the world interesting. If it's not going on within myself, I wouldn't recognize it in a movie. So, we can say then that the world out there is a projection of what is within us.

Then, the serious student says, "And how is that going on within myself?" "And how is that happening within myself?"

When a person can honestly ask these questions and be willing to accept the answers, major changes can occur, and a change of consciousness can happen.

In your hands is the third book of a six-book series, transcribed from the lectures Dr. Hawkins gave in May and June of 2002. We are hopeful that by the end of this reading, you will have deeper insights about these following topics:

Part I

- Context versus content, and how Truth can become distorted

- The world out there is a projection of what is within us

- Everything is happening of its own and everything is perfect right now

- Quantum Mechanics and what it has to do with likelihoods and potentialities

- Prayer opens potentiality to the Infinite Reality

- Spiritual Truths can be heard, yet don't sink in, and how to alleviate this

Part II

- Traditional Meditation: Is this a requirement for spiritual growth?

- The essence of renunciation while living in a busy world
- The benefits of contemplation as a form of meditation
- Letting go of attachments gives greater freedom and peace of mind
- How to go beyond thinkingness
- The most important emotion in spiritual work is that of love, and beyond that, devotion

May the truth of who you really are shine forth as you read this book.

Susan Hawkins and the Veritas Publishing Staff

Map of Consciousness®

God-view	Life-view	Level		Log	Emotion	Process
Self	Is	Enlightenment	⇧	700-1000	Ineffable	Pure Consciousness
All-Being	Perfect	Peace	⇧	600	Bliss	Illumination
One	Complete	Joy	⇧	540	Serenity	Transfiguration
Loving	Benign	Love	⇧	500	Reverence	Revelation
Wise	Meaningful	Reason	⇧	400	Understanding	Abstraction
Merciful	Harmonious	Acceptance	⇧	350	Forgiveness	Transcendence
Inspiring	Hopeful	Willingness	⇧	310	Optimism	Intention
Enabling	Satisfactory	Neutrality	⇧	250	Trust	Release
Permitting	Feasible	Courage	⇧⇩	200	Affirmation	Empowerment
Indifferent	Demanding	Pride	⇩	175	Scorn	Inflation
Vengeful	Antagonistic	Anger	⇩	150	Hate	Aggression
Denying	Disappointing	Desire	⇩	125	Craving	Enslavement
Punitive	Frightening	Fear	⇩	100	Anxiety	Withdrawal
Disdainful	Tragic	Grief	⇩	75	Regret	Despondency
Condemning	Hopeless	Apathy	⇩	50	Despair	Abdication
Vindictive	Evil	Guilt	⇩	30	Blame	Destruction
Despising	Miserable	Shame	⇩	20	Humiliation	Elimination

CHAPTER 1

—

SPIRITUALITY IS TRANSCENDING CONTENT

Well, I'm still on a Walmart high. I was in Walmart yesterday. It's higher than a lot of churches in this world. I've been in a lot of churches in this world. You go into Walmart and everybody sort of drops their persona. Everybody is just who they are like right off the bat. And I noticed yesterday, every single person smiled. Everybody would pass each other with baskets, and they'd just smile at each other; everybody is just who they are. Holy Walmart. Of course, your willingness to be who you are with them brings it out in them. Everybody is looking in each other's baskets, asking, "What, you're having a birthday?" It was really lovely.

You know, in *Power vs. Force* I did remark about Walmart, and Sam [Walton] and I corresponded back and forth. He liked the book. You know, I was looking at integrity in business, and we remarked about the integrity of Walmart, which in those days calibrated in the high 300s. Well, 350 is willingness, helpfulness, good-heartedness, integrity, et cetera. I admired his putting integrity into the workplace, into business, and so we had a sort of mutual appreciation. Now we see that Walmart has become the biggest corporation, the biggest company in the entire world.

Somebody from the *Wall Street Journal* had called me about validity of spiritual concepts in the workplace, in business. And I think Walmart speaks for itself. You calibrate at 380, you become

1

the biggest corporation in the world. Other corporations that calibrate around 70, have gone bankrupt. It speaks for itself, the fact that spiritual principles—as long as you don't call them spiritual—if you call things "God" or "spiritual," you get a negative reaction from a segment of the population. But, as I say, God sneaks in the back door as integrity and integrous business principles because they show up in the bottom line. So, yesterday, the people were saying, "How may I help you?" I mean, wow, what a great space to come from. Who else in the world comes from "How may I help you?" The Motor Vehicle Bureau doesn't, you know what I mean? So, the world, the governments especially, could take a lesson from Walmart, because it's the attitude of being responsible for being friendly and helpful to everyone.

This is the 5th of a series of 12 lectures. The overall design of the lectures is to create a field of understanding of things that historically have been difficult to understand, and to approach it from the side of the ego. So, these beginning lectures have been designed to familiarize us with the ego and how it functions, how to spot the fulcrum by which the ego takes off in one of two directions to create a dualistic perception of the world. So, spiritual advancement, then, is obstructed by structures of the ego, and therefore we plan several lectures on studying the structure of the ego.

In this book, we're going to be talking about context versus content; how truth becomes distorted, becomes almost an editorial style in our society, in which a certain way of distorting reality becomes labeled and given a political title.

There's those on the left and there's those on the right—depends on what kind of experience—so we recognize that in common sense when we talk about the "spin doctors." Just how does that come about and what is the impact on society? So, in our writings and our studies, we look at society as the collective ego. So, looking at the world and looking at yourself, it's a lot easier to look at the machinations of the ego in the world because we don't feel personal about it. It's easy to see it "out there."

So, one way of understanding our own ego is to see how it functions in society. Society is the big model out there. One reason people love movies is you can sit in the safety of your home, and without getting personally involved, watch the vagaries of the ego as it works itself—it's easy to see "out there." So, if we understand something about the functions of the ego, its mechanisms, and its structure, and we observe its functioning in the world, it's an easy step then to see that it's probably going on within myself. If it's not going on within myself, I wouldn't find the world interesting. If it's not going on within myself, I wouldn't recognize it in a movie. So we can say then that the world out there is a projection of what is within us; and studying the world then gives us an indirect; it's easier to accept; it's easier to see out there.

Then, the serious student says, "And how is that going on within myself?" "And how is that happening within myself?"

So, that brings us to understanding that all truth is, let's say all propositions involve two things. They involve content and they involve context. The content is a literal statement. Everyone presumes a certain meaning, but meaning comes out of context. So, the gross distortions of the world that we see in everyday headlines have to do with the failure to identify context. The content is often verbatimly correct as far as most people's logic and reason are concerned, except it's only true within a certain context. The failure is to identify context. This is a fault of science, and all areas of human endeavor. A thing is only true within a certain context, in and of itself. What happens is the speaker or the editorial writer of the newspaper presumes that you will *assume* a context. And that is a very, very great false assumption, that you will assume the same context as they do, because very often, the context that you assume is completely different. You know it's always a joke when I see that some bomber who just killed 52 people and blew up a plane and slaughtered all kinds of innocents, and then he gets arrested. A parade starts for his civil rights. And what about the civil rights of the 3,000 people he just killed? You know what I am saying? Political rights, of course, are what, historically, Americans have died for, but in this particular context, it sounds sophomoric, and it actually ridicules the basic concept [of political rights] by misplacing it in a context that almost invalidates its truth.

Things are only true, then, within a certain context, and the unstated context is where the difficulty arises. Am I making sense? All truth is only true within a certain context. This is recognized in so-called "situational" ethics, in which the ethic depends on the circumstances. Even courts give recognition to the fact that context alters the degree of responsibility—the insanity defense, whether it is willfulness, intention, et cetera. So, the individual, then, is considered to be responsible only within a certain context. We can never presume context. Context always has to be explicitly understood, stated, or made verbatim. The infinite context is what spirituality is all about.

Spirituality is transcending content to realize the context out of which all arises. At the beginning of all these lectures, we'd start out with a statement of what the ultimate, infinite context really is of everyday life. The realization that everything is happening of its own. Everything we see is spontaneously being what it is, exactly as it is this moment. And each moment is therefore perfect. For anything to be what it is at this moment, it has to fulfill the potentiality, which is innate to its creation, innate to its existence. So that if the universe stopped this instant, everything is perfect right now. Each thing is becoming that which is innately its potential. So we see that the rose half-unfolded is not an imperfect rose; it's perfect up to this point. The perfect design is that this rose should unfold in this way, and at this moment it is the absolute perfection of that which has gone before. And that which has gone before is the totality of the entire universe throughout all of time. That's what it took for this rose to be right here at this moment. If the universe stops right now, it's already reached its perfection because its perfection is to be half-unfolded at this moment.

To see that that is the condition, the state of affairs, is what hit me at Walmart yesterday. Everybody was just spontaneously being exactly who they were at that moment, with no disguises; people drop their persona in that kind of a setting. So, the lovingness that's innate within the human condition was able to shine forth. You see that also after catastrophes and all, the shipwreck camaraderie; and when the chips are down, everybody suddenly becomes who they really are. Then when they go back to work on Monday morning, they're back to the same old world-speak! There are two kinds of speak: there's world-speak and truth-speak. And in world-speak, truth-speak is inappropriate. In world-speak, you're supposed to say, "No, I'm not guilty," even though there are 21 bodies lying there. That's world-speak. So we understand world-speak within a certain context. We understand that it's world-speak. Sophisticated people understand it's world-speak; most of the world doesn't. Most of the world thinks it's truth.

World-speak is a provisional accommodation to the practicalities of the everyday marketplace and physical survival. Within ourselves, however, the condition of world-speaking tends to continue. The inner voice continues to lie to ourselves through illusions. And so today, what we want to do is try to transcend those illusions.

One way, the most important way of which we're speaking of today, that illusion arises, is the failure to recognize context. When we judge things and when we judge ourselves, attack ourselves and others, the only way you can do that is by removing it from context.

The only way you can attack yourself for what you did yesterday or last year or two years ago or whatever, is to forget the context in which it happened. So, Monday morning quarterbacking is always fallacious. It's always fallacious why? Because it's a different context. Monday morning's truth is not the same as Saturday afternoon's truth. They are two different truths. The conditions which existed at the time in the past are different than the conditions which exist today. What was accepted worldwide as normal human behavior can't be criticized now in retrospect.

When I grew up, a woman's place was in the home. She ruled it like she was the matriarch. The woman ruled the house. And the man was supposed to go out there and bring home the bacon. He didn't rule the house. He expressed his opinions, but if you liked them diced better than sliced, she said diced is better for you and you got diced. So, mother ruled in the house, and she was revered because she was the sustainer of life. The mother had a profound importance. And as a boy—even if your mother asked you to whitewash the basement on a Saturday afternoon, and you had to cancel your baseball game—if you looked even the slightest disappointed, your father would say, "Wipe that look off your face, young man. It's disrespectful to your mother." Wow. So, the mother had a very high rank. Within her domain, she ruled supreme. And men, when she entered the room, stood up. When the woman entered and came up to the doorway, the man opened it for her. Those gestures were to honor her. Women were being honored.

Initially, the women's movement didn't get that; it was so paranoid it didn't understand that a woman was being honored. It thought the woman was being insulted. Anyway, low self-esteem and paranoia sees insult everywhere. That's the egotism of narcissism: the entitled attitude and the narcissism that undermines, so that you think to be honored is to be insulted. Anyway, the mother reigned supreme. You didn't use any vulgar language in her presence. If you went to a tavern restaurant, there was a separate entrance in the rear called the "Family Entrance." Women never entered the front entrance; that was for the bar and vulgarity. You never saw a single woman at a bar, a woman walking up to a bar. I never saw it my whole life, and the first time I did see it, I was like shocked.

The woman's rank, her status, her worth was revered. Revered. The word *mother* was revered. The mother was respected, revered, and she was also protected. Men went to war to protect the mother and the children. Her function was revered. And let's see what happened to that. Paranoid distortions have fallen upon mother now. So, you see, the context means that when people [missing the context], would say that women had an inferior position, well, this is from Monday morning's quarterbacking, and it's a perception that really misses the entire reality of what went on in those days.

Context Totally Changes Meaning

We can look back at slavery and say, "Oh, how awful that was." Yes, it's awful 250 years later, when it's no longer a world style. In the years of slavery, it was a world phenomenon. All the countries of the world practiced slavery. The Arabic world still practices it. So, you see that by shifting context, we can look at the role, and we can look back and say how wrong it was the way women were held down and couldn't get a job in the workplace. Well, who wanted one? I didn't know of a woman who wanted a job in the workplace. It was thought, when I grew up, that to have the woman of the house working was a disgrace. For a man to have his wife out there working was a disgrace. It meant he couldn't afford to make a living; his wife had to go to work. It was pathetic. Everybody felt sorry for him and he was a "weak sister." He couldn't make enough money to support his wife, for god's sake. She had to get a job at Walmart. So the meaning of a woman's working was completely different. The only woman who worked was the spinster, who had to, and everybody felt sorry for the spinster. So you see how different it's contextualized now. You see what an error it is to go into retrospect, into a different context of relationship and humanity and what was normal and accepted and expected. It was not only normal; it was expected. Everybody fulfilled their social role as it was defined at the time. So you see now, a number of years later, how we can make all that wrong. We can go back 250 years and say how it was all wrong.

We can go back hundreds of years and say how it was all wrong how the Irish were treated. We can say it was very wrong for the Black kings of Africa to capture other people and sell them. So, if you're looking for moral fault, you can keep going back farther and farther into the origination. If there was slave trading, where did they get the slaves? They got them from slave traders. Where did the slave traders get them from? They got them from brokers on the docks. Where did the brokers on the docks get them? They were sold to them by the kings. Where did the kings get them? They got them by inter-tribal warfare. That was the lifestyle.

Instead of killing the victims, they let them live, but now they had to pay back for their life by a life of service. So, from one context, it was all wrong. From another context, the social reality of the time, you can't go back 300 years ago and say such and such was wrong. In the olden days, there were over 500 different offenses that were punishable by death. The reign of King Louis: 500 offenses that you were executed for. So, you see how fallacious it is to shift context and go in retrospect and try to make wrong something that in the context of the time was not wrong. It was certainly not wrong for my mother to be honored, for women to be honored. I didn't feel like I was putting women down to hold the door open for them. I still don't. How can a woman feel insulted if I hold the door open for them? I've had that happen. I open the car door and they say, "I can open it myself." As if I was implying by opening the door that they were weak, and I was superior. So paranoia completely distorts the reality. I was brought up to honor women, stand up when they entered the room, hold the door open. So I'm honoring them, and she thinks she's being dishonored. So don't you see how context now totally changes meaning? Shift context, and you shift the statement to mean the opposite.

This is done all the time. It's been done throughout history. It's the Achilles' heel of mankind that it can't recognize truth from falsehood. So the only real importance of the work I've done so far is to point out that nowadays there is a means by which we can discern truth from falsehood. Throughout all of time man has had no compass, sailing the difficult and dangerous seas of human life without even a compass to tell them truth from falsehood. So it's almost like a new beginning. Therefore, the work we're doing is unique in that I think it's the first time in human history that we've been able to do legitimate, verifiable, bona fide spiritual research.

The only spiritual information we've gotten has been the spontaneous inner awakening of various gurus and sages and saints and beloved individuals, in which it has happened spontaneously, or as the result of rigorous spiritual work. So, we have the information obtained by the subjective awareness of people who've become enlightened. And interestingly, the subjective state of the condition we call "Reality," with a capital *R*, has been the same for thousands of years. There's no variation. Every individual who has reached a certain level of consciousness says exactly the same thing. There's no argument, no difference—perhaps a different style of presentation, speech, be it in Sanskrit or Latin. Whether it's in Sanskrit or Latin or English, the experience is the same.

So, we have the fact that spiritual truth has only been arrived at as a *profoundly* subjective state. Therefore, that which I've stated in books and research and lectures is that the absolute Reality is radical subjectivity. The only way to know anything about any kind of truth is purely subjective. There's no way you can make an objective statement. There's no such thing as an objective statement. An objective statement would be something that exists independent of an observer, and in as much as there's no observer, there could be no objective reality, because there would be no observer to make any remarks about it. Therefore, the closest thing that science and the world has come to being able to make such statements, of course, is revealed now by quantum mechanics, sub-particle physics of quantum mechanics in which the profound role of consciousness is now demonstrated for all to see.

* * *

We can just look at one simple fact for those who are not familiar with quantum mechanics: that as you get to smaller and smaller particles, we discover that there are no infinite small particles that constitute the basic sub-atoms of all things—that a thing can exist either as a particle or a wave, and it's problematic which it will be. And probably the most interesting experiment—which people who don't know anything about quantum mechanics find quite fascinating—is that when you have an atom of matter and it encounters an atom of anti-matter, they negate each other. When that happens, two photons are shot off into space. These photons do not rotate. They go in opposite directions—this side of the universe and this [other] side of the universe, but if an observer looks at this photon here, it begins to rotate. At the very instant that he looks at this photon and it starts to rotate, the photon on the other side of the universe instantly starts to rotate in the opposite direction, even though it's unobserved. The implication of all this, then, is that there is some matrix common to the entire universe which includes both photons within it. This photon does not *cause* this [other] photon to do anything whatsoever. It has no contact with it. Within the macroscopic dimension in Newtonian physics, it has no relationship with it. That field which quantum mechanics comes closest to defining, is what, in spiritual work, we refer to as "consciousness."

When observed, the photon begins to spin, and the photon on the opposite side of the universe begins to spin in the opposite direction just from the act of observation. To merely look at it has a profound effect of consciousness. That quantum space of infinite potential demonstrates how consciousness then can affect the manifest world, because the observation is not measurable in the manifest world, but its effect is. It would explain, then, the space in which prayer could have an effect.

Prayer Changes Context

Prayer changes the context. It has the profound energy within the field of consciousness. So that you might say prayer changes the spin of many photons in the universe. It affects the consciousness of many things and people. So that expectation then has an effect, and we know the common saying in spiritual work, "What you hold in mind tends to manifest." It tends to manifest because you're influencing the infinite quantum potentiality. What becomes manifest is merely a potentiality. So, with prayer and the power of what we hold in mind, we increase the likelihood of this potentiality arising rather than this [other] potentiality and the collapse of the wave function.

It's difficult for the mind which is used to world-speak, the world of the Newtonian macrocosm, the measurable finite world, to make the jump to the nonlinear domain. So, we try to express spiritual reality in terms of a progression from the known to the unknown, from the linear to the nonlinear. We've established the scale of consciousness to try to establish a way of comprehending going from the known to the unknown, and making it more comprehensible in a style of understanding which the mind is used to. A good part of the world refutes the reality of the nonlinear domain and any reality in spirituality, and one reason it does so is that, first of all, it can't comprehend it. The other thing is it doesn't want to be answerable, because with a spiritual domain, it doesn't want to be answerable to a spiritual reality. It wants to be free of that threat, so it can do what it wants to do.

The ego also has another way around that, however, and that is to sanctify sort of a pseudo spiritualization of that which is obviously not spiritual. That's the abuse of the name of God, which we see in today's society displayed to quite an intense degree. The idea is, and a psychotic does the same thing: "Oh, God told me to do it." Well, now, if you can say God told somebody to do something— "God told me to kill her, so I did." So, in the good name of God, I'm starting a "God's name protection society." God has been slandered right and left. Every day's headlines slander God—we're going to kill thousands of people in the name of God. So, God is the great excuse for getting away with murder. And some religions have done it. They call it, "for the good of the faith." For the good of the faith, in the name of God, you can get away with anything—anything, because once you cite God, then all rules of human morality dissolve; and that allows you to be free to do anything you want. When I have a patient that hears God talking to him, it's dangerous, because they can and will do anything. Anything the voice happens to tell him.

Lower astral entities have learned this over the millennia, that all you have to do is to tell the listener that you're God and you can run them like a machine. The lower astral domain is made up of those spirits who have refused God. Not those who are unable to recognize God, like atheists. Atheists are integrous. They're the ones I asked if there's a place for them in heaven, and it said yes. To say that, "in all due honesty, I can't really get what God's all about," is just being honest. It means that "I'm not that evolved yet. It's not a reality to me." That's an honest statement of truth. You get to come back here and keep moving on until it does start to make sense to you. But it's a good starting place. It means it's at least in integrity.

No, the lower astral is those who were given the choice and refused God. That's a totally different can of worms. And we've noted in doing the spiritual research, a lot of times a writer at one time, at the time they did their writings, their writings calibrated a certain number. And then the teacher, somewhat later in life, calibrates at a considerably lower number. It's as though one rises to a certain level of awareness in consciousness, and that summons forth a test or a temptation or a challenge. When you make a spiritual statement about your spiritual reality, it's almost as though you pull up from your own unconscious, a challenge to that statement. Many living today and many living in the past, many living in the far distant past, much to our astonishment [calibrate lower in later life]. So, because we're in a way, the first ones really doing this kind of spiritual research, it's sometimes somewhat challenging to us what to do about this discovery and to assess what the impact might be on the world, or socially, to discuss certain things.

So, in a way, this group to whom we speak and the readers of the things I've written, were really the first ones in history to look at things, you might say, to look at subjectivity objectively. That's a mastery of a turn of phrase. To take an integrous way of using an integrous means to examine that which is difficult to understand and which has been confused over the centuries. Now, the confusion over the centuries has been at great cost to mankind. Mankind pays a huge cost. We're not talking about academic niceties today, some kind of a lofty intellectual viewpoint. We're talking about the mistakes that'll cost you 40 million lives. One mistake, one leader—30 million lives. How often? Very often in my lifetime.

Chairman Mao totally miscalculated the human psyche. He didn't realize that the human brain has a reward system, and without the reward system people are not going to work on a collective farm. Chairman Mao's agricultural experiment caused the greatest famine in history; 30 million died of starvation. Stalin killed off another 30 million in the gulags of Siberia. Hitler killed off 70 million. We're talking about more people getting killed than the entire population of the United States, just in my lifetime. And these all come about as the result of distortions of truth in which context has been disguised or falsified. So, what we're talking about is not necessarily an academic nicety at all. We're talking about survival of entire nations, entire continents, practically. You can wipe out a whole race of people with one distortion of truth.

Now, because man couldn't tell truth from falsehood, he was like the lamb waiting for the slaughter. All you need is one fancy slogan. A bunch of students throwing rocks at the barricades—there you go! Every revolution is started by a bunch of stupid kids throwing rocks at the police, so they can get the police to fire. Once the police fire, you've got a dead student. Camera! Dead student! Propaganda's value is tremendous. Always get the snipers to kill a kid. You need a kid in every propaganda shot. You live in a place that is attacked by the enemy, and hundreds and thousands are killed. What do you do there? You send your kid to school in a school bus right between the snipers, right? "Have a good day at school, kids!" You live there, folks. You move your grandparents in. Oh my god, and now we're supposed to feel sorry for you. You see the manipulation that goes on, endlessly: endless manipulation, the endless distortion, the endless energy that the ego gets out of this, the energy of being right. Righteous indignation is addicting. The world loves it. The world lives on righteous indignation and mutual provocation, so that you can fall back into righteous indignation and be the martyr. And now, hate, and of course, what you do, is you keep out of awareness the context in which all this is happening. And what is the context? The context is that you're causing it. That's it.

So, taking responsibility means to stop creating a false context. It's because of keeping context and content carefully separated, that all the catastrophes of the world have come about. So, what we're talking about today is basic, you might say, to *all* human suffering. The game of playing martyr, the game of provoking other people to be the attacker, the narcissistic ego game of entitlement. It's out of entitlement that all these phenomena arise. First, you have to misconceive, then you have to have sufficient egotism out of which comes entitlement. And now you'll feel entitled to do and carry out within the world a distorted perception of reality. It's one thing to see America as a great Satan; it's another to feel entitled, therefore, to bomb innocent civilians. So, entitlement then gives the permission for the action. Entitlement, then, which in the end, entitles you to eventually go to the lower astral realms. You're entitled, all right! Oh, God, I just realized that. So, because your political philosophy is so incredibly wonderful, now you're entitled to enslave, to use the guillotine, to send them off to the gulag, to put them in chains. So, the dangerous part, then, comes from the entitlement of the megalomaniac, who is always an excellent demagogue. The demagogue then uses this distorted reality, plays upon the ignorance of the masses, but the real severe action, then, is in the extreme entitlement. Slobodan Milošević, we've spoken about him before because he's such a perfect example. When you watch him on television, you see the supreme arrogance of one who feels that their own ego is actually God.

So, the basis of the ego, then, is that it assumes that it is God. And the megalomaniac refuses to accept that there is another God, which would threaten the divinity of one's own self.

What we said today really has a profound impact in understanding human history. Understanding the evolution of human consciousness as it is revealed by civilization and the history of civilization. We see the evolution of the ego and how it expresses itself in today's society. I'm not talking about ancient history. The reason I like to use things from today's headlines is because it's staring you right in the face now. I mean in my lifetime I went through all these hundreds of millions of people being slaughtered all over the globe. And I was a witness to it. So, we're not talking about things that are abstract. We're talking about things that are extremely real to, really, the majority of mankind as of today.

A Way of Validating and Confirming Truth

Well, what I've been sharing with you is an evolving field of knowledge, you understand? We've found an instrument that opens whole realms before [now] inaccessible. A way of validating and confirming truth, a way of discovering things that mankind has never had before. Mankind dealt with the limitation of logic. Logic is in the 400s. One of the great impediments to enlightenment, the 400s is probably the major block for an enlightened group.

We talked about context. The unsophisticated person presumes that the rest of the world thinks the way you do. I got news for you. The rest of the world does *not* think the way you do; in fact, the rest of the world thinks you're stupid. The world is not run by logic and reason. All the political disasters, military disasters throughout history, including this very day, are based on the presumption that the other people think like you do, hold the same values that you do, are restrained by the same moral constraints that you are. Nothing could be further from the truth: reason and logic, fairness, and humanitarianism are ridiculous. You think that stopped Chairman Mao, Adolph Hitler, anybody? "Oh, they wouldn't do that because they'd be killing themselves." Remember the Cold War? "Oh, they wouldn't do that. They'd be killing their own people." Killing their own people was the *specialty* of megalomaniacs. "The Germans *deserve* to die," Hitler said. Saddam Hussein, all the megalomaniacs of the world are run by megalomania. Megalomania means that the people have no value, whatsoever, except to serve their [megalomaniac's] vanity.

No, the opposite side will not be constrained by that which is reasonable—at all. They will kill all their own people. So, when you realize that, you realize how dangerous they are. They are not constrained by reason and logic. So, we'll talk about two things today.

The research is evolving continuously. And you are part of it, by being here. Sometimes a question will come up—we haven't looked at it. We look at it right here and now, the first time it comes up. Many of the presumptions throughout mankind's history have never been challenged. Many of them are being challenged, for the first time.

We're talking about context. You cannot look at yesterday's events and make it wrong because the context is different. Part of guilt is looking to the past, attacking ourselves for what we did, said, thought, or felt at that time. But at that time, the *context* was different. Today, the context is different. It only looks wrong because you're making an error of context. To treat women now the way they were treated in the late 1800s would be a social error. It was not a social error then. We were talking before how women were treated when I grew up. When I grew up, it was an agrarian society. Most of the population lived on farms. You didn't survive without the woman. The woman's work was critical. It's one thing to bring in a couple of hay wagons full of corn; it's another thing to turn it into food. Men left by themselves could starve to death right next to [the produce]. It's a lot of work to get it from here, to there. Bringing home the bacon is one thing; making it happen for you and your family is quite another.

So, we can't make things wrong by retrospection. You can't attack yourself for yesterday because the only reality is right now. People say, "I can't stay in the now; my mind wanders to the past or the future." That's an absurdity, because your mind can only wander to the past or the future, in the "right now." So, you're still always in the right now. It's right now you're worrying about the past and the future. You are in the "now," folks! So, you can't get out of the now. All you have to do is appreciate what the context is of that state of "now."

So, the fallacy of shifting context is done in politics all the time. A statement which sounds good as a street slogan is now put in a different context of an international event, and now you come from moral righteous superiority. What you don't realize is that you're being sophomoric, and God save us from the sophomores. God save us from the sophomores because they live in academia. They were at the college age of naiveté and they stayed there and became a professor. The world "out there," they haven't the slightest contact with. I know, because in the practice of medicine, you would not believe the BS that comes out of academia via government regulations. You say, "Where's this guy lived all of his life? Has he ever seen a sick patient?" I mean, get with what's real! You know what I'm saying? There's new regulations called HIPPA. They run perhaps 58,000 pages, and of course, I'm responsible as a physician for knowing every iota on every page. And if I don't, I'm subject to $250,000 fine and 10 years in prison. I mean, is that friendly? Is that like Walmart? The government agencies calibrate at 202. You know what that is? That's perfunctory honesty, because if you aren't, you get arrested! 202. I don't want to get into the government right now.

Hearing the Truth Is One Thing; Having It Sink In Is Another

We read all the spiritual material, or we go to church, we listen to a great lecture—we feel terrific. And the very next day we curse the first guy that cuts in front of us in traffic. I say to myself, "Didn't I get it or what?" So, to hear about it is one thing; for it to sink in is another. The only problem you've got is allowing it to sink in. What keeps it from sinking in? Many of you, I'm sure, have spent years reading spiritual literature, hearing erudite speakers, going to holy places. I've been to all the holy places, folks. Yeah. And yet, a thing will remain the same. You say, "How can that be? How come it doesn't sink in? How come I don't get it? How come I'm not transformed by the wonderful truths I've heard?" I don't know. It seems to be a great block, isn't it?

We're willing to be loving toward all people. We noticed that in Walmart that happened. Everybody was friendly. Yesterday I was coming down the aisle and I had a bunch of blank videotape things, and I was going down, and this lady looked sweetly at me and she said, "Oh, pardon me," and she pulled out of the way. How come everybody is so sweet and loving in Walmart? Now, on the street, she'd say, "Grrrr!" like this and go right ahead. So, it must be certain context allows the truth to sink through. I don't know what it is, why it doesn't sink in: "Why it doesn't sink in has to do with an unconscious resistance of the ego—resist." (True.) "It's an unconscious defense mechanism of the ego—resist." (True.) "It's the ego defending its very structure—resist." (True.) The ego is defending its very structure. To allow even *one* truth to shoot through is the beginning of the end for the ego. "That's correct." (True.) So, the ego defends itself by not allowing any immigrants. If it gets one sweet, loving little old lady wandering through, you've blown the whole game, you know what I mean? "Iris, you're not supposed to be treating the people this way!"

"Consequently, Love is the greatest danger—resist." (True.) Ah, yes. Oh, I got it, okay. "What I just saw is true." (True.) That's what we're building up to in the lectures, anyway.

We're approaching it from the side of the ego, because when we get to lecture whatever-it-is about the heart, I don't want the heart impeded by the structures of the ego. So, first, we're disassembling the ego. The ego becomes weaker just by recognizing it for what it is. It already loses its divine authority. We're removing the divinity of the ego. The more we describe the machinations of the ego, the quicker it is to see it; the weaker it becomes. Because when we get to the lecture on the heart, if I am capable of giving it, the heart now sweeps through, unimpeded, because the paths of the ego's resistances have been weakened.

That's the beauty of *A Course in Miracles*. The beauty of the *Course in Miracles*, when I saw it, I said, "Wow, brilliant!" *A Course in Miracles*, first it takes you through an elimination of the ego structure before it comes up with truth. As I say, Lesson 76, "I'm only subject to what I hold in mind," only works if you've done 1 through 75. I said, one time, I think it's Lesson 76, around in there—I was talking about the students I had in *A Course in Miracles* who wouldn't go weak with anything, and I tracked some people who were just starting the *Course*. And of course, fluorescent lights made them go weak and all that kind of thing. And around 76, fluorescent lights and all the stuff that makes everybody go weak with kinesiology, no longer [did]. It was about the lesson, "I'm only subject to what I hold in mind." Somebody heard that, and he read that lesson, in hope that his asthma would be cured the next day. I said, "You forgot the first seventy-five lessons, folks. [Lesson] seventy-six is meaningful if you've gone through one through seventy-five." "Oh, okay." Why? Because it changes the context; so, that's what we're doing here.

We want to get the ego dead to right, so that when we get to the heart, its way will be unimpeded. All right.

People have heard of the truth for their whole lifetime, and it's had no effect on them whatsoever. I had a lady I know well. She said, "I've gone to metaphysical groups, discussions, weekend retreats, and for thirty-five years, nothing's changed!" That's curious. It's also sad, isn't it? It's also an area for research then, isn't it? How can you go for 35 years and not have anything change? Let's see: "That's possible." (True.) "That still exists in the same lady—resist." (True.) Oh, my God, it still exists in the same lady. It's been 10 years since she said that. All right. "So, the cleaver that will cut through, then, is love—resist." (True.) Okay. It's only love. The only thing, then, that can weaken. . . . Oh, I get what it is. The only thing that can weaken the ego's structural resistance to maintain its total defense from letting any spiritual truth come in then—the only thing that can do that defense is love. So, out of love, then, one accepts what one has just heard as truth. It was out of love for my father and my grandfathers that I adopted their view of reality that women were to be honored. It was because of my *love* for them. Reason couldn't have proven it. Women try it all the time. It'd drive you crazy. You wouldn't arrive at that by logic.

So, out of love then, out of love. Maybe that's the effect of the teaching. Oh, let's see. Somebody asked me that question. What is that question? How does the calibration increase from watching videotapes or audiotapes, as compared to being here in person? I don't know, we never asked that.

"The calibrated energy of the teacher is innate to the videotape—resist." (True.) Okay. "It's innate to the audiotape—resist." (True.) "It's the same as the presence of the teacher—resist." (Not true.) Let's see how that can be. "Divinity doesn't record on videotape—resist." (True.) Oh, I see, because it's out of form. Okay. Videotape can only record content [form], within the Newtonian paradigm. It doesn't record the infinite divinity out of which the totality of Reality arises, which is reflected through the teacher. Okay. "The teacher reflects that." (True.) "The teacher is reflecting today." (True.) [Speaking quietly while testing]: "Over 800." (True.) "900." (True.) "990." (True.) "995." (True.) "999." (True.) "1,000." (Not true.) All right. It is radiated through the consciousness of the teacher. That's the value of it. I'm a little disappointed. I thought it recorded on videotape.

What happens is, you hear the teacher, and that allows your own divinity to come forth. So, the radiance of divinity is felt from within: "That's true." (True.) Okay. "Right now, the vibrations of the teacher create the context," (True), "which brings forth the response from the listener's context." (True.)

Okay. So, then, what it does is it removes the blocks. What we're trying to do is to disassemble the ego, so the radiance of the Self shines forth—which it does. So, the difference is, the presence creates a certain aura, but it's the listener's divinity that allows them to realize the truth of what's being said. So, the truth of what's being said, then, becomes acceptable by virtue of love. When my father and grandfathers spoke about this matter, the ring of validity was absolute. There was no question. "Don't you ever speak that way to your grandmother." That was it; you don't question that; you don't ask about it—that's the way the world is. All right. So, I see what it is. What could undo it then, would be the respect for the love out of which the truth was spoken. I see that, okay.

Someone once asked me, "How do you see the perfection of twenty million dead bodies lying there?" You can see it in the rose. Can you see it after a nuclear disaster? If the perfection of "All That Is" is there at all times, how come it looks the way it looks at times? We said as the rose is unfolding at every instant, it is already complete. At a certain state of realization, every instant is already complete. There's nothing you want; there's nothing you need; there's nothing you desire. As you get to the end of the movie, the TV set stops; you don't feel any loss of how the movie ended. Every moment is complete up to that moment. There's nothing to look for, seek, or desire; nor is there anything to regret. If you live in the moment of now, there's nothing to desire and nothing to regret because everything is already perfect, including getting blown up. It's perfectly fine to get blown up.

Everything Is the Perfect Expression of That Which It Is

Everything is the perfect expression of that which it is. A hundred thousand dead bodies just blown up by an atomic explosion is the perfect expression of *that*. Bin Laden's bombing of the Trade Center is the perfect expression of calibrated energy of 70: "Correct." (True.) It is correct. That's what 70 looks like. Calibrated level 70 is the age of the dinosaur—rapacious, bloodthirsty.

So, anyway, everything is the perfect expression of what it is. The dinosaur is perfect, rapacious, greedy: "looking only to myself and what I want; nothing else out there has any rights." It takes what it wants and kills what it wants in the process. That's the energy level 70. That's Bin Laden and the World Trade Center.

The consciousness of mankind, don't forget, has been below 200—which is the level of integrity, which is just common decency like the IRS throughout all of history. It's only in the late 1980s that it went to 207, went over 200. So, mankind is the perfect illustration of that which is horrendous. Mankind up to now has been the perfect demonstration of that which is horrendous. Mankind is *the* demonstration of that which is non-integrous and horrendous. The history of the churches, the Inquisition, the endless wars, the Hundred Years' War. . . . In my lifetime, I've already lived through I can't tell how many wars already. I was born right after World War I, so it's been 40 million here, 30 million there, 40 million there—with some political slogan to justify it. Watch out for the idealistic political slogan—it's killed more people than anything else, hasn't it?

So, each thing then is the perfect representation. You see, if you live in the instant of the moment, you only see the bullet coming in and going out his back and the blood spilling all over, and it's like a dance. He is the perfection of getting killed by a bullet.

That's how you get killed by a bullet; that's how it happens, folks. It's like how you chop your thumb off—in one instant, it's absolute perfection. That's the perfection of cutting your thumb off like that. That's the Zen of catching chickens. The Zen of catching chickens in the henhouse. In one instant, with absolute clarity, the hand got that chicken with no "me" involved. The hand grabbed the chicken. There was no block in the intent. No hesitation. It was absolute perfection. Got that chicken! When you need a chicken caught, you're looking at the world champion chicken catcher! I didn't get it in karate lessons. I knew it was there, but it seemed to take too long—it took forever. I knew that moment would open up through karate, but instead it opened up in the chicken house. That moment of absolute light, where there's no personal self. It was the perfect expression of that which it was at the moment—as a caught chicken.

So, everything is being perfectly what it is, at the moment. Hitler was the perfect demagogue, and he was profound. You look out there over the masses and look at the History Channel of World War II, and you see hundreds of thousands of people going in this great parade with all the flags and the music. I mean, it was fantastic. The *perfect* expression of nationalism. Perfect. And then you follow nationalism through to where it takes you. After Leningrad, half a million dead Germans; dead bodies being dragged back by oxen and God-knows-what. That's the perfect expression of what nationalism is.

So, we can understand the political person who objects to nationalism. It says that history's been horrible. That's correct. Nationalism is not patriotism. Patriotism is something different. To confuse nationalism and patriotism is a grave error. There's one of those errors of context. Nationalism is one thing; patriotism is another. Patriotism comes from the heart. The reverence with which we held women as I grew up came from the heart. Feminism is like nationalism. It's a political position. In my opinion, there's no heart in it. There's no love for women at all. It exposes them in the harshest terms and the harshest structure.

So, patriotism is expressed in the poem: "Breathes there a man with heart so dead, with soul so dead, who never to himself has said, 'This is my own, my native land.'" Now, what you're talking about is the truth of the heart. Truth of the heart has no politics in it. Nationalism will kill you. Love for one's country is a totally different thing. Let's see: "Patriotism calibrates over 500." (True.) "510." (True.) "520." (True.) "530." (True.) "540." (Not true.) Patriotism calibrates at 540. "Nationalism calibrates over 200." (True.) "205." (True.) "210." (Not true.) Nationalism calibrates at 205, 210. "So, the feminist political position calibrates over 200." (True.) "205." (True.) "210." (True.) "215." (Not true.) See, "political position" is only 210.

The reverence for women, out of which they were held as I grew up, calibrates in the 500s. So, it's not necessarily progress to go from 500 to 200. Now men slam the door in your face and say, "Look, fight for yourself." Take the downside of the workplace. Inviting people into the downside of the workplace is *comme ci comme ça* [neither very good nor very bad]; it's got its upside, it's got its downside, but you can't hold that one as the moralistic high ground. What we're talking about is the imposition of the supposed moralistic high ground, a political imposition on the psyche of society, which is vulnerable and naïve. It's vulnerable and naïve because it doesn't understand context.

That which is of God brings peace and love. So, you can tell instantly that which is of God—it brings peace and love. That which arises out of the love of God—because we're building up to the lessons where we're talking about love—it's the love of the truth, that begins to remove the obstacles to its acceptance. A person has gone to many, many lectures and intellectually gotten it, and nothing has changed. So, the ego has no defenses against love, really, except denigration. So, I'm mad at feminism as a political stance because it puts women down from over 500, to 210, but this is a lot better than 190 or 180, which is true in some countries.

So, you see context spells everything. Is that an advance? It all depends on the context from which you're coming. That which comes from God is love. Love calibrates over 500.

Having a tool for consciousness research allows us to investigate a lot of the premises of society, a lot of the slogans that we unconsciously accept, a lot of the invalidations of reality. If love is the biggest danger to the ego, then that which is loving in society would attract attack from that which is against love. That which is threatened by love will try to attack love.

So, we watch these phenomena, then, throughout society. We see how they're disguised as political positions. See, it's not really political. "Political" is just a way of looking at a thing. A thing is not its description, which is very hard for the intellect to see. The "thing" is not what a description of the "thing" is. The description of a thing is only a description of the thing. And the "thing" is something else.

The "thing" is here. There's a certain sophistication in quantum mechanics in that it says, it doesn't call "reality" measurable anymore. It calls it "observable." In quantum mechanics, it doesn't talk about measurements—eight foot by six foot. In quantum mechanics, which is the most advanced edge of science—it gets closest to spiritual reality—there's only observables. So, the reason it's quite advanced is because now you have intellectual sophistication, an awareness of the limitation of the intellect. Traditional science, God bless it, has brought us all kinds of wonderful things. Its limitation is, it does not realize its own limitation. Quantum mechanics is the leading edge of advanced theoretical physics. It describes observables. It's only what you can observe. The measurable is one thing; observable is another, because observable retains the *observer*; that the observer is present, not just the measurement existing by itself, but the observer now has an influence. So, all we can say about society are what seem to be our observations of it; the same with the ego. So, when we talk about it, we're not talking about a self-existent reality, we're just talking about observables.

We have used kinesiology as a tool to cut through between measurables and observables as a way of going from one paradigm of reality into another. Let's see: "Mother's Day when I grew up calibrated over 400." (True.) "450." (True.) "500." (True.) "510."

(True.) "520." (Not true.) Mother's Day calibrated about 520 when I grew up. I wonder what it is today. "Mother's Day today calibrates as a social phenomenon over 450." (True.) "460." (True.) "470." (Not true.) [Level] 470. It dropped from 520 to 470. Intellectually, we say, "Oh, yes, Mom's the greatest, the most wonderful, et cetera, et cetera." But as a social phenomenon, it dropped from real reverence. See, the reverence is the realization of the divinity coming through the feminine. The divinity which comes through the feminine, which was the basis of the reverence, see. We revere that which we intuit the divinity of its essence. Before the woman was obscured by political slogans and stuff, we saw her for what she was—the reflection of God as nurturance, as the very essence of love manifesting within the human domain; so, she was held in reverence because of the reality of the divinity of her existence. That's what Mother's Day's about. The recognition of the divinity out of which arises existence, the existence of the magnificence of the feminine. A guy can try to be a great mother, but I tell you, folks, it's a fake. You're trying to be the good father bringing the bottle there, but it's not really a thing, you know what I'm saying. "I've got a new compressor at home, and I'm dying to go up and try out my new compressor that I got for Christmas," but you're supposed to be the good father and feed the baby. It isn't really real, because it's not rooted in the evolution of human society throughout the eons. It's not rooted in me to nurse the baby. I think it more tends to be rooted in the mother.

So, each thing then represents the perfection of that which it is. The unfolding of the rose when it's half-unfolded, the battlefield full of slaughtered troops, the dead civilians after the atomic blast. Each thing was exactly what *that* is. It is a demonstration, the dramatization of that level of consciousness, and that's what drives man. Some people get that it's not too good, that a battlefield of dead people is not too good. Not everybody gets that. A lot of people think it's wonderful, victorious, and we'll go on to the next battle, but somewhere in the human psyche, they get that this is not good. So, the evolution of human consciousness, then, is built upon what we would now look at from a calibrated level of 430, as disasters and failures. But that's Monday morning quarterbacking. At the time, the victory seemed incredible and wonderful; we've conquered the "Gauls" and converted them to Christianity or whatever the hell we did; it's a great victory, a great victory. If you calibrate the energy of that, we'd see it's probably around 120 or something.

So, we can't Monday morning quarterback ourselves as a civilization, as humanity, by looking back at the dreadful past. Unvarnished, the past is, frankly, quite dreadful on the level of the collective. On the level of the individual, not necessarily so. In the home those who are quite loving calibrate in the 500s. But society as an evolving collective, as you can see right up to the present day, is different.

View It as a Learning Curve

So, what we're looking at is the learning curve. So, when you put yourself down for the past, something you did yesterday or didn't do yesterday, whatever—all you're looking at is that you're looking at a learning curve of where it was then. That's where the learning curve was then. Where you are now is not the same place. So, guilt, shame, attacking yourself, regrets, all this kind of thing, have no validity in reality because the *context* is what gives the reality its reality. Let's just see: "It's context that gives reality meaning—resist." (True.) Okay. So, content has no meaning whatsoever. What does a dead body mean? It doesn't mean anything. If you live long enough, you walk over a lot of dead bodies. All kinds of sizes, shapes, ages. Dead bodies by the carloads. What does it mean, though? Oh. What does anything mean? It's context, then, that gives everything meaning. It's the divinity of the Self, that within you, the Self with a capital *S*, shining forth as consciousness, the Source of your own existence. So, that's where we find God. You've looked into the fact that you exist. How did it come about that I exist? Well, in one of the first lectures we tried to transcend that ignorance called causality, because the ego would say, "Well, it's caused by genes and chromosomes, and sperms and eggs and all kinds of biologic peculiarities." There's nothing more peculiar than watching a sperm and this egg doing their thing on TV! That's where you came from? Yep. Did Louis XIV come from that? Yeah, it's biologic reductionism. No, that isn't what you are—that sperm and egg—it's not really what you are at all. We find out from kinesiologic research, in fact, that the spirit doesn't even enter the embryo until the third month. Let's just verify that again: "That is a fact—resist." (True.) So, for three months, it's just a small animal, potential animal embryo there. The human spirit doesn't decide that this is suitable for a life experience until the third month. No, the embryo is up for option. I never asked about how they figured out on the other side. "Okay, George, it's your turn." Bong, it's a George now!

—

CHAPTER 2

FAITH, REVERENCE, AND TRUST

So, what we haven't mentioned so far, we said, truth only, meaning only comes out of context. One context that we haven't spoken about this morning, of course, is karma; that you have both discernible context, undiscernible context, and non-identifiable context called karma. That's why much scientific experimentation doesn't make sense when they come up with contradictory results because they don't define the context. The reason computers can never create an artificial intelligence, they can only do logic trees. Human intelligence is a subjective evaluation of an infinite number of millions of data of information which it intuitively wends its way through, without actually processing. The reason you can't do a computer replica of human consciousness is for one thing, the major portion of the context is missing. It can only program content. One piece of context is not available to put on the computer because it's unknown, is karma, no matter what you say; and that which is in the unconscious. So, all you can put on the computer would be that which is reasonably logically recallable. You cannot put what is in the unconscious because, by definition, it's unconscious. If it's unconscious, it is not available data; you can't put that in the computer.

Context is nonlinear; computers only deal with the linear. Therefore, meaning, significance, value—you can't put Mother's Day on a computer. Because of the reverence—how do you put reverence into a computer logic series? You can't. Why? Because it's a feeling state; it's a way of being with; it's a way of being with the totality of that which you are and the totality of the feminine. The way this consciousness is with the feminine evolved over eons. It evolved over *eons*. Its reverence for the feminine is *eons* old. That cannot be put into a computer. So, it is context that gives a thing meaning and value, significance. Our spiritual work, then, derives its power from the context, the willingness to trust the words of the teacher.

We said you can go to metaphysical lectures for over 35 years and never change one iota. It's because the person has denied the power within them. It is the power to transform the world, the world of the word into the subjective experiential world of spiritual truth. The power is within you. Where does the power come from? The power comes from willingness; willingness about what? There was the willingness to accept that women were to be revered when my grandparents said that. My father said it. There was no resistance to that. No resistance.

So, there was trust. There was trust in the words; there was trust in the sincerity with which they were said. There was trust in the integrity of the speaker. So, out of love for the source of the information, all resistance was relinquished, and that was accepted as truth incorporated within for a lifetime.

The same thing should then ideally happen with spiritual work. The power of the consciousness of the teacher, the educator, should be sufficient as one's trust in it is profound, like it was in my grandfather. Then the resistance dissolves itself. If I tell you that the feminine is infinitely divine, worshipful as the expression of God in that expression; you know that's the truth, is it not? Is that the truth? Then you reverence that within yourself, the feminine within yourself you reverence as the expression of God as it expresses itself in the feminine. As it comes out of form, the Divine begins to take on attributes which we eventually recognize as form. The difference between male and female, divinity has already come into form as male and female. Because tomorrow is Mother's Day, I'm concentrating on the feminine and the magnificence and the beauty of divinity expressed as the feminine.

So, our acceptance of that doesn't depend on it being accepted by other people. It makes no difference to me how other people hold women within their psyche. It's their problem. There's no conflict and no problem with the way it is within, as close to its Divine nature as possible. So, what did the grandparents do? My uncle, all the men in the family held women in reverence. Why was it so powerful? It was because they were holding it as close to its Divine origination as possible. They were holding it as a condition, not as your aunt or your grandmother or your mother as personages, but they were holding it as a powerful field of realization. And I got it, I *got it*; I got what it was. The divinity innate *within* the feminine—that's what I got. That's why it is worthy of reverence.

So, our resistance in incorporating truth and instantly recognizing it, the resistance to it can be bypassed by faith, love, the trust, and openness in the divinity that we intuit as the field out of which the information is coming. It is out of infinite love that that is forthcoming from consciousness into the awareness of the listener. It doesn't take 35 years of attending lectures. It takes one instant of trust; one instant of trust. One reason we use kinesiology is to clear the obstacles to trust. If I tell you that the expression of motherhood, and this calibrates at 540, and the way women are held by a political position, if we calibrate those levels, that sort of removes the doubtingness of the intellect. The intellect is the great doubter, and the great blocker to truth.

So, we try to also handle the ego at the same time. So, all that I have ever spoken of became an absolute reality in one instant, 35 years ago or whatever it was, somewhere in the long distant past. All that I'm saying today became an instant reality. That's what speaks right now. What speaks right now searching for how to express that so as to bypass the resistance of the intellect, the mind, and the ego, and you see, as I saw as a boy, the incredible magnificence of the divinity of woman. One instant. My grandfather said, "You never speak to your grandmother that way." I got it. I got how she was held.

So, it takes one instant to get what you're looking for—not 35 years. It only takes one instant. In one instant, the ego lets go its resistance out of faith, confidence, and trust. That's what it does. When my father said that to me, I knew he was not lying. I knew the truth. So, all resistance stopped, and that became incorporated in truth, the truth of my own reality.

So, I'm going to use personal experience to demonstrate a certain principle. The last thing I want to happen is for people to read these lectures and then tell me nothing's changed, that nothing's happened. "I went to all these lectures and nothing's changed!"

So, you might say, in a certain context, then, that I belong to you. Everything I'm writing belongs to you. Is that so? Yeah. So, what am I, then? The spiritual educator. In other words, we share with you the truth as it was subjectively experienced, and as it is present within, huh? But that's not comprehensible, so we go back to what it is that keeps it from being comprehensible. We try to explain it in terms that are understandable to the scientifically trained mind. We have to pay attention.

Jesus wasn't dealing with scientifically trained people. They couldn't read or write, for God's sake! He had a snap of a job. They hadn't read all the books; there weren't any books around the whole thing, you know what I'm saying? No, things have evolved in the last couple of thousand years, and the listener, the student of today, is somewhat different—considerably different, far more sophisticated, in the 400s. Those people there that Jesus dealt with were probably in the 200s, right? "We have permission to ask that—resist." (True.) "The key followers were below 200 to start with—resist." (True.) So, it was the power of the truth coming through that transformed the people, and the people instantly saw the truth that he revealed. That was his authority, out of which they became enlightened. The saints all became enlightened as a result of the capacity to drop all resistance and just respond to that truth—just as I did with my grandparents and my father about who women really were. And I got it in an instant who they really were. I didn't need to read any books on the subject—just *got it*, right off the bat. In one instant, I got who women were.

When you walk through Walmart and you smile at somebody, they get it as a gift to them. Do you notice how they light up? You ever walk through Walmart and smile at people? Everybody lights up all the way down the aisle. Just try it. You probably never noticed it, but she's pushing this, and you're pushing that, and you look over and smile at her. It knocks them out. She's so happy that somebody smiles at her and recognizes her, that she just beams right back to you. It's like instant love all the time. I used to do that in the streets of New York City. The streets of New York City are like Walmart. I lived in New York City. I would just walk down the street and just love everybody as they came along. People just beamed. They just loved it. You could stop anybody on the street in New York and start talking about anything. "What the hell do you think about Mayor So-and-so?" Instantly they would give you a talk. It's like you had known each other for 30 years. There's no barrier there; I love the streets of the city of New York. You can stop anybody and everybody's a character, and it's terrific. The dialect, the whole style of what it means to be a New Yorker; there's a certain implicit understanding of it. The rights and wrongs—under certain circumstances it's not really stealing—"he left it out," you know. It's a totally different change of context. "He left it laying there." Well, okay, he left it laying there. Even a judge wouldn't convince you, probably—he left it laying there—a whole different context of ethics and morality.

So, what is acceptable there is not acceptable here. The context of New York City is different than the context of elsewhere. Do you understand that? The context makes it different. The context makes its meaning and its significance become different. So, context defines meaning and significance. To do the same thing here that would be nothing at all in New York would be ethically a different animal altogether. He can't just take his change and not feel guilty about it. "Well, he left all his change on the bar, you know what I'm saying? He went to the bathroom. What do you expect—that it's going to be there when he gets back?"

We've tried to approach it from the viewpoint that the ego as a totality will not tolerate any infringement of its boundaries because it realizes that it's a threat to its totality. It's an interlocking system, and to let in love means that the end is inevitable. Let's see if that's so: "To allow in love means to the ego, ultimate dissolution—resist." (True.) Above all else, then, the ego fears love. The ego's scared to death of Mother's Day: "The ego is scared to death of what Mother's Day really is—resist." (True.) It's scared to death of what Mother's Day really is.

The recognition of the divinity of love in its expression, of course, on Mother's Day as the feminine, would mean that love as a prevailing dominant value would infiltrate all of society. And that would be the end of many corporations, and political positions and all. Therefore, yes, the ego's scared to death of Mother's Day. I don't know if it's scared of Father's Day—we'll wait until June.

Love Is the Greatest Threat to the Ego

So, love then becomes the greatest threat to the ego. The way to not go to 35 years of lectures with nothing happening, then, the secret of it is love. The secret is love for the truth. The secret of it is faith and confidence and the integrity of the source of the truth.

And one means of accomplishing that is by kinesiologic testing. To what degree you can trust the validity of what is being said. It comes from the energy field, the calibrated energy field of the speaker. The love of the truth, then, because truth is only meaningful within a certain context. And what is the context of the words that have been said? We could test the truth of "Deutschland Uber Alles," and then we could test the context out of which it came. The consciousness of Adolph Hitler. Actually, Adolph Hitler played upon . . . the evolution of fascism in Germany arose out of a philosophic position, a professor, it's in my book [Professor Karl Haushofer, please refer to *I: Reality and Subjectivity* (2003), Chapter 4: The 'Ego' and Society, pages 70 and 71]. It justified the German invasion by a doctrine of *lebensraum* (living space), that Germany had the right to invade neighboring countries because it needed room to live. That was a weak one, huh? But the whole structure came out of that "room to live!" That's what I transmit to fellow drivers on the highway. I need room to drive, folks. Therefore, I have the right to crash my car into his and knock him off the road because I need driving room! That's a rather weak intellectual position, isn't it? Did we ever calibrate that? "Deutschland Uber Alles [retained as the anthem of Nazi Germany, along with the Nazi party anthem] calibrates over 100." (True.) "110." (True.) "120." "130." (True.) "140." (Not true.) [Level] 140. "Adolph Hitler at the time-we have permission—resist." (True.) "Calibrated over 120." (True.) "130." (True.) "140." (True.) "150." (Not true.) They corresponded, huh?

So, the demagogue finds the downside in human nature and knows how to directly appeal to that. The smart politician knows what the consciousness level of mankind is, and that he can easily summon up that hatred. He knows that hatred is there, only waiting to be summoned up. At the opposite end, we know in spiritual work because of the reality of existence itself that the capacity for love and to enlightenment is also available within mankind. So, we'll leave hatred to other people who know how to summon that forth.

And all we want to recognize here is that divinity is the source of your own existence. It is out of divinity that consciousness arises. Consciousness is the field holding us all together, out of which everybody is able to hear and experience that which is being said. The presence within all of us is what allows us to experience the subjective experience of that which we are and which we're trying to verbalize here.

So, Reality then is a radical subjectivity. We'll get to a lecture on meditative techniques and all, but at all times the shortcut to God is to merely realize the infinite presence of your own capacity to experience, and the source of your own existence. Nothing has within it the capacity to create its own existence [out of what comes existence itself]. We bypassed causality as a plausible explanation, I think, in the first lecture; we knocked causality on its butt! The world hasn't heard of that yet, but the days of causality are over. Because the ego will say, "Well, what about causality as an explanation?"

Everything is created in such a way that its essence unfolds due to the divinity of its source. It's because of the divinity of the source of creation that all things are perfectly what they are at any moment. That which appears catastrophically awful appears that way because it's out of context. Because of who you are in the present, that looks terrible in the past. That's already a judgment. The awful, manifesting its awfulness is supposed to be awful in the awfulness of its awfulness. And it's perfectly awful in the dreadfulness of its horrific ugliness and horror. Despicable! It's supposed to be that way, so you know what it is. Now you know what it is. And then we choose differently this time. We look at the dead bodies on the battlefield. We look at the runover children. And something within us begins to change.

But it changes so slowly, doesn't it? Calibrate yourself the consciousness level of mankind century by century by century—190, 190. You say, "Wow, didn't mankind learn anything?" The War of 1812? One war right after another! Hitler was really so stupid! He was really stupid. Napoleon had just pulled that trick and blown it. He went around and did the same thing—invade Russia. Eastern and western front at the same time. You say, "How can anybody be so stupid?" So, that ignorance and that stupidity that we're trying to find our way through today.

The Buddha and Jesus both said, "The only sin is that of ignorance." Sin has a moralistic putdown. It is really useless. It's using guilt as a hammer to beat people to death with, or to beat yourself to death with. It says there's ignorance. Ignorance seems to be innate, then, in the structure of the ego itself. How can you go to 35 years of lectures and not get anything and still be the same person? There's something within the ego itself that accounts for this. Century after century, millions slaughtered. Go to the next century—would it be better? You'd think so. No, it's still 190. Millions more slaughtered, still 190. Millions more slaughtered. You say, "Whoa, there's something that's really thick-headed about the ego." There's some innate stupidity. There—we got it today:

the ego is just stupid. It really is dumb. So, we should treat it like an imbecile. Stupid. Dumb. Pitiful. We should feel sorry for the ego. It is so dumb; it can sit there for 35 years and not get it.

The source from which you are learning or hearing, or . . . something, has to be of a certain dimension to break through the resistance. I held my grandfathers with reverence and respect, and my father and my uncle. Because of that, I didn't argue. And it was appropriate to the way women were treated, was appropriate to the way that they were held. And they showed me how they were held. And the reason it rang true is because it was based on spiritual reality. Yes, the feminine is the expression of divinity in that genre of human expression. And I got it in an instant.

The same thing should happen in any spiritual literature, spiritual teaching, whatever. The respect, the letting go of resistance to the truth of its source. What is the source of its truth? The source of its truth is the presence within that speaks. Classically, what's speaking now would be called, in Sanskrit, "Purusha." Purusha would be the essence of the Self of the teacher which is expressing itself. That's what's expressing itself. It has nothing to do with the body that it's using at the moment. It could use anybody. Can't trust Purusha; it will grab anybody, speak through anybody; it can get there.

The source of the realization of the truth of all spiritual teachings, then, is the Self within you. You have within yourself the power of recognition. It's only then, recognition. If what my grandparents had told me, my grandfathers, my uncle had told me, was not innately true, it would not have rung; it would not have resonated within. It's because of the presence of truth within me [that] I was capable of hearing the truth. It is only because of the presence of truth within everyone here that there's any capacity to extract any truth out of the research that we've done in the last year that I am sharing with you.

* * *

We've got enough questions to keep us busy for a while. Well, each question reflects what we intend to talk about anyway, and it just reminds me what we're going to talk about. The disassembly of the ego takes eons of time. Most people in this audience have probably been here 50 or 60 times before, to try to accomplish that which happens within an instant. I use the word *happens* linguistically, to make sense. To sense one's reality is simple. It's only a matter of knowing where to look. If you look over here, you're looking at the written word. Thirty-five years of the written word. Where is what you're looking for? You can all sense, right in this instant, right in this instant there are people already destined, like you, to become enlightened. What you do is, you catch the experiencing of the world just prior to the mind's commentary about it. If you back off from the mind, you find an inner stillness which hasn't said anything yet. You live in this space before the world has said anything yet. When you walk outside, you're struck by the beauty of the surroundings. You haven't said anything about it yet. You live in that space. This space is pre-verbal, prior to mentalization. The difficulty with verbalization is one has to come out of that space and come forward into that verbalization because that's what the world expects. You have to do world-speak or the world doesn't understand because nothing's being spoken.

* * *

Right at this moment just sense within yourself that which hasn't had a second yet to make any comment about what the speaker is saying, yet. The mind's commentary is a delay, there's a split-second delay, and you live in that experience before any comment. When you dive off the diving board into the water, there's no thinkingness about it as you hit the water. The thinkingness comes later, a split second later that that dive wasn't made correctly. Ow. That's a split second after you go, splat! on the water and realize that full gainer was only a three-quarter gainer. The red-belly express. Ow!

Even as you think you're not getting it, you're there right now. Right now, within everybody's consciousness is the presence of consciousness itself, prior to any kind of content. So, you draw back, and you live in the space right before the mind starts to make commentary. You hold back in this space beyond the mind's thinkingness. Thinkingness should be voluntary. I think when I'm forced to think, the world is forever asking you to think and comment, and there's no *end* to it. You're always exhausted by coming out of infinite peace and beauty of silence because the world has some dumbbell question. It's like the radio I grew up with. It's got a dial, and you turn the dial. That's it. The world hates that kind of radio, I guess, nowadays. Somebody gave me an electronic radio, a new radio, and it's got a 14-page manual—I can't make it do . . . I can't even get it to tell time. I've got one I don't know what to do to make it even tell time. You get dragged into this complexity. It pulls all your energy and your interest, and your survival gets pulled "out there."

Ramana Maharshi said it correctly; when I read Ramana Maharshi, I said, "That's it." He says the mind gets pulled into the world away from the Self. And one's reality is prior to the Self. One's reality is prior to the Self, as what? As a condition, as a field. So, your reality is a field, an innate field out of which is just prior to thinkingness; when you wake up first thing in the morning, you do not even know who you are yet. You don't know what your name is. You don't know where you are. All is just the awareness of awareness itself. And, at that point, all you know is that you're awake, period. You know that phase when you wake up? You know you're awake and that's it. So, that's what the condition is that you're looking for. It's always present. When thinking that I am that which is talking and thinking is what's real, the identification of self, of reality as the ego—when that goes away, in an instant there's deadening silence. Then the question is, how to be in the world of dead silence when the world is talking all the time. It's hard and took many years to adjust how to do that. Most people, when they go through that space, don't readjust. They do not reenter the world. It's some kind of karmic momentum and some people do return to the world.

So, at all times, you're really making an effort to come out of the state of inner peace. It's sort of like having to wake up and deal with the world. Look within yourself and see there's really a reluctance to deal with all of this thinkingness and judgmentalism and emotionality. It's exhausting. Within yourself, you'll find, "I'm really tired." I'm exhausted from dealing with the world. Aren't you? That's why people look forward to dying. I can't wait until it's *over*. I mean, it drags on and on and on; and you know what the end is anyway. So, what's the big deal? Now or later, it's all the same, isn't it? Which brings up the question on Alzheimer's.

Somebody asked me about Alzheimer's. I have dealt with Alzheimer's a lot the last 5 or 10 years. In Alzheimer's, the spirit leaves—starts leaving. That's all it is. You're [as spirit] not here anymore; you're like an enlightened person. You ask an enlightened person, "What's today's date?" What the hell does he care what today's date is? He doesn't live in today's date. There's no date in Reality. There's only the experience of nature being what it is. If I go and ask a tree, "What's the date?" It doesn't live in the world of dates. It doesn't *live* there. The tragedy of Alzheimer's is in the witness of Alzheimer's. The suffering is in the witness. When you don't know what the hell day it is anymore, are you suffering? No. I've asked a thousand Alzheimer patients, "How are you?" "I'm fine." Then they make up stories to make you happy. I mean, you obviously want an answer from them. So, they'll make up a story on the spot and five minutes later, they've forgotten the story.

Do you fear Alzheimer's? No. Why? Because people identify with the content of ego itself, and there are people who are frightened to death of losing their memory. What the hell if you don't remember 1932 to 1934? I mean, what's so precious that you would want to be able to recall it instantly? Right? Anything? A person says, "I'm afraid I might lose my memory." I hope you do—I mean, nothing better could happen to you! Memory is the recall of perceptual illusion as it compounds it over the years. I mean, it's like the poisoned well, folks. It's killing you. So, do I feel sorry for the Alzheimer's patient? No, I feel sorry for the witness, the family.

"Poor old Granny's losing it." They're weeping and sobbing. Is Granny weeping and sobbing? No, she's not.

How is it here in this nursing home? I went to all the nursing homes in Yavapai County, close to 10 years. Every day I knocked my brains out. There were not many doctors who would go see them, so the county was happy somebody would make a house call and go to the nursing home and talk to these sweet old ladies. They're all adorable. I loved them all. It's because you can see what's lovable has been completely preserved. What's lovable is totally there. What's irrelevant has disappeared. All they've lost is what's irrelevant. As you get closer to the end, some people have the—let's not even title it anything. The spirit begins to leave before the physical body. Some people, by the time they physically die, the spirit's left years ago.

I knew Bill Wilson, who was the founder of AA, and Bill would say—I actually treated him the last years of his life, with vitamin E, red ginseng, antioxidants we were fooling around with. And he would drift off, and then his watchers would be concerned that Bill drifted off. "How is it, Bill?" He'd say, "You know, there are many places you can go in heaven." He'd been visiting in heaven back and forth, like he was shopping for a future residence.

What you see in old people then—do I fear Alzheimer's in myself? No, I don't fear Alzheimer's in myself. At 75, I have senior moments, however. Yeah, I call a lot of people "what's-his-name." "What's-his-name" and "what's-her-name." I know who they are. So, what happens then, is that which is important and significant is no longer located within the ego's function. It's not important to be able to figure out—to read this manual and figure out how to push all these buttons so that I can set the watering system for every third day, and half-time on rainy days and three days—I looked at one in the store the other day, a new watering system thing. It was mind-boggling. It has so many bells and whistles you couldn't figure out how the hell to make it water the lawn. It would serve 12 stations. Twelve stations? I just want one that turns it on and off. They're on at three, off at four. Don't you have one like that? "No, we don't have one like that." I'll tell you, folks, the easiest way is, in the morning on your way to work you turn the watering system on. You turn the hose on, sprinklers, and when you come home you turn it off. Is that simple or what? Just saved you 72 dollars. Oh, you can turn it on and off yourself! Never thought of that! After breakfast, you turn it on. Before dinner, you turn it off. That's all it takes. Reality, then, is the world of simplicity. The person with advanced Alzheimer's is ultra-simple. They have no needs, no wants. You say to them, "How are things here?" "Fine." How are they treating you? "Fine." Would you rather be someplace else? "No." While you're still hanging on to the mind in the past, you grieve. But as, happily, Alzheimer's progresses, you lose that attachment to the past, and now you're not grieving that you're not living on the farm in Michigan anymore.

Except for the witness, subjectively Alzheimer's is probably closest to enlightenment than most human consciousness. "That's a statement of fact—resist." (True.) Yes. I used to look at the Alzheimer patient and I thought, "Christ, he's a Buddha; what's his problem? He's got no problem." They're living in the instant of "now," in which the Self is still present, but it's only present as Self with a capital *S*; it's not present as a small *s*. So, Alzheimer's is the dissolution of the self with a small *s*; and those who are more spiritually advanced see that the Self with a capital *S* is still vitally there. They're just as loving, warm, friendly, responsive in the instant.

That's what we summon forth in Walmart. See, when you lose your identification with your persona, you're just walking with a basket and you're a nobody. This [other] person is also a nobody. These two nobodies can instantly be very friendly and quite loving with each other. Isn't that true? If you're walking at Walmart and somebody bumped into your basket and suddenly she started to cry, you'd say to her, "Hmm," you know what I mean? Because that veneer that prevents us from realizing who we are, has been removed.

So, Alzheimer's from a certain viewpoint, then, is a blessing. You forget that you're dying, so you don't have to even grieve that. If you know you do not have Alzheimer's, you've got to worry that you are dying. If you've got Alzheimer's, it doesn't even enter your mind to worry about it. The whole thing is effortless and painless, and I think on the other side you'd hardly notice the difference. As you go on the other side, do you notice the difference? Oh, yeah. You notice the body is lying there. Anybody that's gone out of body realizes that. You realize, "Oh, where's the body?" It's lying there in the bed. "Oh, I forgot. I thought I was still that body." So, helpers come to remind you that's not yours anymore; you don't need it anymore. You don't want it anymore anyway; it's a mess. You leave it at 93, blind, deaf, dumb, crippled with arthritis and one leg missing—I mean, who's going to hang on to it?

So, that's my view of old age, suffering and death. The suffering is due to hanging on to what "was" and the absolute refusal to surrender. Death and dying, Alzheimer's, are moments of great opportunity to reach spiritual enlightenment. They're great moments because investment in the world, investment in the mind, the investment in the functions of the body and the mind have diminished to the point that it's easy to let it go. Easy to let it go—to be in the space just prior to thought.

So, your reality is the sense of presence, your sense of being here. To hear what he's talking about isn't necessary to really understand it. You sense that you're present. You sense that you're in the presence of the presence of the Allness of it. It's like when you walk out in nature. Just before your stupid mind says, "Isn't that a beautiful tree?" you catch the space in which you saw the tree's beauty without comment. That's the space you live in. It's just prior to thought. It's easy to just fall back into it. It's not like something you'll have to accomplish through years of studying meditation. The willingness to trust it, and just drop back into that, back into that, that is your reality. Reality is *a priori* to any programming. What is it in the computer world? The software and the hardware. Okay, so your beauty is the hardware which is always present prior to hitting the button and getting the software. "Oh, isn't that a beautiful tree?"—is too late already when you said that. However, even while you're saying that you can back off from the ego and not identify with that statement. So, the two things exist, reality with both context and content. The two things exist. One can realize the foolishness of the statement, and simultaneously, be aware of the beauty of the woods, prior to any comments.

Q: *"How should we hold the situation in the Middle East, coming back to the present world?"*

Well, the presidency of the United States calibrates around 450, and it has throughout the centuries. I think a few of them, of course, in olden times were higher—but in modern times, the average consciousness level is about 450. I think Roosevelt was like 499, or something. Churchill is 510. The consciousness, then, of the leaders of the modern world are usually in the mid-400s. They're going to do what appeals to reason, the intellect, intelligence, research, their advisors. They're going to pull together the best advice team, and then they will give it a slight preference due to political position. The current president has no problem with right versus wrong. Right is right, and wrong is wrong—what's the problem? Within that context, it's true—within that context. Now your question is, should that context apply? When a tiger is about to rip your jugular vein out, the context is a little different than looking at a tiger in the zoo. The context is a little different. What's permissible? The alternatives are somewhat different, depending on context. So, it's the context of the zoo that makes it a little different than the jungle.

I've been asked a lot of questions about calibrations of levels of consciousness. See, calibrating levels of consciousness is only a tool. It's a way of getting information. It doesn't get you enlightened. But it does tell you what's a dead end—what's a dead end and also what's a pitfall, what to avoid, which way to go—so it's helpful as far as direction. Of course, the capacity to tell the truth about anything instantly brings up a zillion questions about everything. So, you have to look at the intention behind the curiosity, behind the question. Very often, you find out more about what you wanted to know by examining the reason why the question is coming up. It's been a unique opportunity because we've found out that there is access to the field, to the field that accounts for the spin of this photon in this direction; instantly the spin of the photon in this [opposite] direction, and the only thing that changed was human consciousness observed it. Human consciousness does nothing but *look* at this photon and keww! instantly the photon rotates this way; this [opposite] photon rotates this [opposite] way, instantly. No connection between the two whatsoever. The only connection that's possible would be that there's a common field, a field common, a matrix, a latticework. I think it's called in quantum mechanics hypothesized a matrix, a latticework, something that under which the whole universe, the reality of matter, the reality of all that exists, arises out of that which is invisible, indefinable, undefinable, unlimited. It's that sense of that within yourself. It's just a matter of sensing it. It's a matter of intuition. You go back within yourself to that which is there prior to hearing this word. There is nothing there right before this word is heard and right before the mind thinks of a reaction to the word. It's in that space. The most likely place in a situation to find that space that we call "Enlightenment" is while you're eating cookies. If that don't take you there, nothing will.

We've been asked to test a number of various things. Many of them I already know the answer, but just for fun: "A near-death experience tends to break down the ego—we have permission to ask that question." (True.) I don't think it is correctly phrased. "A near-death experience helps one transcend the identification with the ego—resist." (True.) "It can bring about major transformations in consciousness—resist." (True.) "It can bring about a major positive leap in consciousness—resist." (True.) The way you tell an out-of-body from a near-death experience, and there's a lot of lack of sophistication, not only in the general public, but even some spiritual teachings. Out-of-body is one thing; near-death experience is another. Out-of-body doesn't necessarily change your calibratable level of consciousness at all: "That's a fact—resist." (True.) Yeah. You can go out of body and come back in body, and boy, that was really interesting, but there's really not a major shift of consciousness. The near-death experience is of a totally different dimension. One is just awe-struck by the immensity of the realization of the nature of divinity, and that that which you're experiencing is not different than that which who you are. So, it's a major transformation, near-death experiences. So, to tell the truth, you can calibrate before and after the experience. Out-of-body, you usually will be about the same. However, out-of-body, you do become more sophisticated. You realize that you also have an etheric body. One thing that you're quite certain of as you are floating in space, is that you have an etheric body, because now you're it. Out-of-body is, of course, quite exhilarating. It happened to me many years ago and in those days, nothing was heard of it. I think I have recounted it before. In a serious illness, suddenly there I was, five or six feet over the body, looking down at the body in the bed. And the interesting thing was the sense of self went with the etheric body. The capacity to know, feel, think, hear, reason, everything; the sense of "I" was up here, and *it* was down there. So, it is an opportunity to realize that the sense of self, the spiritual self, is an energy body and not a physical body.

At the time, I don't think it had any particularly transformative experience. I told my psychoanalyst about it; I was in psychoanalysis at the time. God bless him, dear Doctor Ovesey. I said, "God Almighty, there was this experience." "You had a toxic psychosis there with a reduplication of the body image and a rejection of one aspect of it." I said, "You're right, you're right." We were both atheists; he didn't think much of God, religion, and at the time, I didn't either, so we didn't have any problem with it. Yes, there were a toxic couple of irritated brain cells. That's all we knew about it in those days.

We've got some interesting leading questions into subjects which we were going into anyway. In my talking about women, of course, I was just using Mother's Day as a point of reference. I'm not differentiating men from women, because divinity, of course, is equally present. The form that it takes within the perceptual world is different. I mean, a man is different from a woman within the physical world, you know what I mean. And symbolically they represent—it's symbolically in the unconscious. Those of you who are familiar with the work of Jung and all, realize that the archetype of the feminine and the archetype of the male are two different things, and historically they've always been, even the planets are named with various genders and the gods and all. That's really a different subject. It's a subject of study in itself; the origin of how this arises, how it expresses itself. The divinity of all is the same, of course. I was just talking about its expression as a woman and then using that to denote the importance of context; how woman was conceived of in the 1800s, early 1900s. Now there's a shift of context, but the Reality, of course, has not been changed at all.

I read somewhere that the IRS Regs [Regulations] run 58,000 pages, and of course as a taxpayer, you are legally liable for knowing all of its contents—you realize that. Because it's unknowable, the government can't understand it, so it makes you responsible for knowing it. Yes, so, that's the intellect gone wild, without any limitation.

So, ranking would be the mind's proclivity for its status and things like this, and then projecting it onto these fields. Nothing is better than anything else. It's different than something else because it's addressing a whole different problem. Is loss the occasion for grief? Or is it the gateway to freedom and elation? It depends on who you lost. So, you see, you don't have to *mourn* loss at all. Let's say you own a whole herd of cattle and they're all dead by morning from a terrible disease. Well, now you don't have to get up and milk them, I'll tell you that. Four o'clock in the morning in the Midwest through the snow and the ice and pitch-blackness, with snow up to here, and walk through all that cattle poo to milk this thing.

Every loss, then, can be recontextualized as an opportunity for freedom. As valuable as that possession may have been, it still gives the opportunity now to discover a new life. The company collapses, you lose your position—is that a loss? It is only if you hang on to the past.

Why? What's really going on is you're afraid of the freedom that the dissolution of that commitment now opens up. You're now free to become anything you want, go anywhere you want.

Are you going to stay in the same part of the world, same part of the country? It's sort of scary, the immensity of the freedom that you have. So, ranking then would be just a projection that we project onto this. And the question often arises, "How do you see perfection in any and all conditions?" Because perception is a projection, and you'll find what you're looking for. That's the whole basis of quantum mechanics. That's the reason they stopped calling things "measurements." What is found is the consequence of what you're looking for. The observed is, then, seen as a function of the observer. The observer is what determines what's observed.

What's observed depends on intention. We said that the calibrated level of consciousness, as well as karma, has to do with spiritual intention. Now, spiritual intention doesn't fluctuate. It tends to move quite slowly, although you can have a major event such as a near-death experience where spiritual intention suddenly takes a giant leap. The moment-to-moment little angriness, irritations, regrets, all these things, those aren't fluctuations on the level of consciousness. Level of consciousness is pretty steady. It's set up by the karmic development of the totality of your spiritual commitment. So, the spiritual commitment then tends to prevail. Fluctuations may occur only in a fleeting thought. If you calibrated a thought, the thoughts may jump all over, but that which you are doesn't change that easily. And people involved in spiritual work know how difficult that is, to get it to change. So, it's pretty much set and determines how you see the world. That calibrated level of energy is influenced then through your own decision.

Is it influenced by the group? Yes, I think so: "Your calibrated level of consciousness is influenced by the group with which you identify—resist." (True.) It's influenced, because you're saying, "I am that; I embrace that as my reality." So, it isn't so much the group as that you are verifying that the group represents your own spiritual goal.

Not killing innocent children may be a very important spiritual learning down here [low on MoC]. There are certainly very large religious groups in the world right now where getting up this far [to the same low level on MoC] is a great advance. Getting over

70 is a major improvement. That God is not pleased by your killing thousands of innocent women and children would seem so ludicrous to us, but it might be a tremendous aha to somebody.

So, as you move up, your own spiritual awareness moves up, the group that you find useful at one time, you can outgrow the group. Eventually you outgrow all groups. So, the group is useful as mutual support, and the continuous feedback helps to clarify one's understanding of that particular religious position or spiritual position. And then one moves on.

I think we spoke—there were a number of different groups people asked me about individually. I don't like to do them publicly. You see, "by their fruits ye shall know them." We don't have to ask what the calibrated level of certain groups and their actions because "by their fruits ye shall know them." So, we did write something about the difference between a true spiritual group and a cult. Cults calibrate below 200. That's the quickest way. A cult is non-integrous. So, the cult may take the name of a great leader or avatar or spiritual guru, or whatever, and call itself that; and then, underneath the guise of that really become a political action group.

The one in China that's having trouble with the government, its problem is that it didn't stick to just strictly spiritual; it got political. When it got political, it began to challenge the Chinese authority. All governments, by nature, protect themselves. That's why they're your government. So, China outlawed them [Falun Gong]. So, if you stay home and meditate and do good works, the government will not take any position about you. But if you start getting out there with a parade and you're going to overthrow the regime, and put in your philosophical concepts, prepare to die. You know, prepare to die. You can make a grandstand statement, but that isn't what makes the world turn.

So, a cult can take on the name of a great leader, call itself "The Holy Church of God." And in the name of Holy Church of God, burn down the homes of whatever. Just because they call themselves that, doesn't mean anything. So, we define the difference between a cult and a truly integrous spiritual group. Of course, we as a group know all you have to do is to calibrate them.

That which is of God gives forth love and peace. It's as simple as that. Love and peace is what radiates from it. Sometimes the originator or the original speaker of the spiritual truth is loving and pure, but then that's grabbed by other groups who then run with it and use it as justification to convert people by the sword. Jesus meant the "sword of truth." He didn't mean the sword of steel. So, it's misused then for other ends.

We noticed that people are born at different levels of consciousness, the very instant of birth. And there's another question having to do with geography. I meant today to have a transparency to project with a world map by showing—calibrating the various levels of consciousness in prevailing civilizations over the world. It's very interesting because you see that like tends to attract like. That's sort of true. So, if you're born with a level of consciousness of 50, you're very likely to get born into a body that happens to be part of a civilization that in general, calibrates around 50. In other words, it's like nothing happens by accident. Like tends to go to like. At the very moment of birth—at the very moment before birth even, the calibrated level of consciousness of the entity is already identifiable, and we can actually calibrate it: "What we just said is true—resist." (True.) That's a fact. We've done it over and over. So, what we think is unspiritual—let's say we look at the lifestyle of somebody here [low on MoC], and we go, "Cluck, cluck, cluck." Yeah, but that person came in here [lower on MoC], so for them to be at 100 or 150 is a major advance. Major advance.

We can look back at previous lifetimes, and these areas that you transcend become very, they stand out of that lifetime, the lifetime of surmounting physical death. It's thrilling. You commit hari-kari and ecstasy! The second you're out of body—ecstasy! Surmounted that for all time. Never again to be inhibited by the fear of physical death. That makes a very ferocious warrior who's not afraid of death. Look out. So, from that moment on, you've perfected the fearless warrior. You can walk into a hail of bullets and you don't give a rap about it; no longer susceptible to that. Now that you've transcended that level, there's no point to having to get myself killed over and over to get the point. You have a physical body, see the thing laying there, the other spirit, and you laugh at each other—"Great job, Joe," "Great job, . . ." We both did it. So, there's really no point to do that again. You don't have to commit hari-kari 10 or 12 times to get the point of it. It's not pleasant, so I would only do it once if I were you.

It isn't that one thing is better than another. As you grasp the totality of consciousness as it evolved throughout time, and the way it manifests on this planet as the evolution of life on this planet evolving into mankind, evolving into modern man, you begin to realize what you're dealing with. You're dealing with like a profound morass, out of which consciousness is only just barely popping its little head. It didn't cross 200 until the late 1980s. In other words, it's like modern consciousness is just being born *now*. We're probably part of the birth process of *Homo spiritus*. *Homo spiritus* is a declaration made by this great, wonderful being here: "*Homo spiritus* is correct—resist." (True.) "It *is* the emergence of *Homo spiritus*—resist." (True.) In the book *I: Reality and Subjectivity*, then I say, there is now emerging out of this morass of negativity, ignorance, and finally the 400s—the ego, the appearance of love, which is relatively recent in the human condition and the prevailing energy. We have now the emergence of the spiritually aware being. Aware of themselves as a spiritual reality. The emergence of *Homo spiritus*.

All the branches off the evolutionary tree . . . it's not a linear thing, where this [one branch] gets better and better and better and better. In the evolutionary tree—evolution, by the way, happens on the level of consciousness. Then it manifests within the physical domain. But you see its branches off the tree. This branch goes off here. This branch doesn't just get longer and bigger and better. No, it stops there. Its potentiality has been realized when it hits the perfection of that which it is. And then, you see later another branch off the tree, and then another branch higher off the tree. So, the evolution of consciousness as it's expressed in mankind is *not* the continuous evolution of one trend at all. It's the emergence of a new trend.

Those of us here today represent, really, a new branch off the evolutionary tree. We are not an improvement on Cro-Magnon man. We're not an improvement. We aren't an improvement on *Homo erectus*. *Homo erectus* went here [on a branch by itself], and it got as far as *Homo erectus* could go—end of *Homo erectus*. Each of us, then, represents a branch off the tree, the new branch off the tree, called *Homo spiritus*: "That's a fact—resist." (True.) That's so. And the group here certainly represents that which is *Homo spiritus*. The awareness that we're more than a physicality, the awareness that we're more than a mind. The recognition of the spiritual potential within, which is only to be discovered and nurtured for it to flourish and blossom. Did Neanderthal man worry about these things? No. Not suitable. I think Cro-Magnon man was about 70. That has to do with physical survival as an animal, to get enough to eat, to mate, to stay alive. So, that's the animal. So, you had to first perfect the ability to maintain life within animal form, within biped form, and then consciousness went on. Consciousness got bored with that one.

What we see now is where the evolution of consciousness is at its present moment, this moment here. The evolution of human consciousness throughout all of time, throughout eons and eons of time has resulted in us. We're it! We are it, Amen. We are it. The advancing edge of consciousness is really what is here today, is it not? What is the ultimate Truth, how does one reach it? The tools that are useful for the task is where the advancing edge of spiritual consciousness is.

Is it possible in the old religions? Well, religion is one thing, spiritual truth is another. Hypothetically, at least in the beginning, they are one and the same. But we see throughout history how spiritual truth then gets destroyed for secular means and original truth is lost within. A more spiritually advanced person utilizes what they realize as the spiritual truth from that religion and lets the chaff go. Whether you eat meat on Friday or not is really irrelevant to God. Let's see if that's a fact: "That's a fact." (True.)

Okay. When I grew up you didn't eat meat on Friday because it was respectful—well, no, it was a sin, really—it was worse than respectful. High Episcopal, it was like Catholic—you didn't eat meat on Friday. It was really out of respect for the religion, a respect for the teaching. Whether it got you in or out of heaven, I don't know. But as a kid, I suppose I would worry that if you ate meat on a Friday and died, you would think you would go to the other place.

"We have permission to do some public leaders—resist; they are in the Middle East—resist." (True.) Okay. I myself have wondered about this particular individual. "We have permission to calibrate him in public—resist." (True.) He's on TV every night, so I guess he's not too timid about who he is. "This gentleman calibrates over 200—resist." (True.) Wow. "Over 220." (True.) "230." (True.) "240." Wow. (True.) "260." (Not true.) "250." (True.) [Yasser] Arafat, 250. Let's see. "Arafat *was* at 250, ten years ago—resist." (Not true.) No.

Now, Arafat is interesting because we see a lot of well-known and in fact, currently popular gurus that wrote books years ago when they were in a high space, usually in the mid-500s. And the books calibrate in the high 500s. But if you calibrate what is the energy of this entity today, you often find they're like, 130. Common. Very big-name gurus in the world. Everybody goes, "Oh," when you mention their name. You calibrate them, and they're like 140 or something. It's because they went up, and then were hit by, you might say, their opposite and succumbed to the opposite. That's how the cult is born. You have a certain charisma. People start to follow you. You start to believe your own publicity and start getting power over others. You start telling them what to do. You develop a cult. You have to swear an oath; you've got to pay money and get a thing on your whatchamacallit. And every time you hear the name of the leader, you bow. You know, this is true for even EST [Erhard Seminars Training], God bless EST. It was Werner [Erhard], right. It was Werner everything. You go to an EST event, there would be Werner, about bigger than the theater, on the screen. It was all Werner, yeah. On the other hand, EST taught some terrific things. With EST, you could take off weight very easily, you know, lots of good things in it.

So then, the cult, you see, somebody asked me about various things I said I don't want to calibrate them in public. The leader becomes charismatic in a cult. He becomes all Baba So and So, Master So and So. Master Baba. It all becomes Master Baba with many "oohs and aahs," so it's like a personality cult. Then there's a specialness to belonging to the group. There's a group form, it gets a name, maybe an initiation ceremony, and now the group becomes—you're either with them, or not with them. You're one of us, or you're not one of us. So, it becomes very special—instead of seeing yourself as part of the All, the Allness of life, you now become partitioned as special. Special. So, if you're a member, that makes you special. Then, there's group lingo which is only known to the members of the group. There's a specialness to the cult leader. There is a negative reaction if you leave. If you decide you're going to leave the "Holy Rosary of the Round Table," or whatever, horrible things happen to you—snakes in your mailbox and hate mail. So, there's a negative reaction if you try to leave. So, you like become a prisoner. So, it's really brainwashing is then proceeded about this organization, about its specialness; often it's considered yourself exclusive. Some go so far as to say they're the only ones that are going to get into heaven. It's a little hard to imagine, but there are people who believe that. There's a specialness, a uniqueness, a cult-like atmosphere, a specialness to belonging or not belonging; various titles go with it, and after a while, there's probably a lot to be learned. There's a lot to be learned at that level. But, then at a certain level, you begin to realize that this is not freeing and liberating, this is confining. This is confining and it tends to be totalitarian. At its greatest expression it becomes totalitarian. At that point, your intuition will tell you it's time to move on. It's very often hard to see because the adulation with which certain people are held by large groups. So, mass hysteria, the suggestion and madness of crowds takes over. So, if you're in a group and everybody is going, "Heil Hitler," you find yourself repeating enthusiastically, "Hei-." So, the charisma of the leader, then, becomes magnetic, and the adulation of the group tends to be infectious. So, you've got to watch that you don't get brainwashed.

The only thing a teacher can do is reflect truth. It doesn't make them special, unique; anything at all. Don't forget, to a realized person, their condition is just nothing. It's just the way it is. Is the cat's condition, to a cat, special? No. It's just being a cat! So, a true teacher is just like a cat. It just is what it is, but there's nothing to say about that. It's just being what one is. So, there would hardly be any adulation expected from being what you are. The cat doesn't expect me to say, "Oh, Great Cat," because you're a cat. The presence within is so powerful, It Is, of itself. It Is, of itself. It bypasses all personhood. So, there is no one to go, "Ooh and aah," over.

Helpful Reference in Regard to War

Q: *"Can wars be prevented?"*

The preludes to war are highly visible, as can be seen in such pre–World War I political ideologies as Marx and Engel's *Das Kapital* and *Communist Manifesto*, the political writings and speeches of Lenin, Hitler's *Mein Kampf*, and Chairman Mao's *Little Red Book*. The Nazi occupation of Europe was justified by the political ideological concepts of *lebensraum* (living space), the political ideologies for which were provided by Professor Karl Haushofer. These were later combined with the philosophy of eugenics to justify genocide.

Political distortions are usually those of context, class, or displacement in time or conditions. For example, as society evolves, what was considered normal at one time is later considered to be detrimental or unacceptable and redress is then called for. Financial or military recompense is demanded of the current citizens to compensate for what is now retroactively considered as victimization in a past era (e.g., Hitler's play on the "unjust" Versailles treaty). Inasmuch as everyone now living can be conceived of as suffering real consequences of some past condition, there could be constructed, therefore, a defensible view that all persons currently living are "entitled" to recompense for the past ignorance and mistakes of a more primitive civilization. Injustice can be cited anywhere in past times [*I: Reality and Subjectivity* (2003), Chapter 4: The 'Ego' and Society, pp. 70–71].

Let's go on to Mr. Sharon. [Ariel Sharon, prime minister of Israel, 2001–2006]: "We have permission to do Mr. Sharon in this group at this time—resist." (True.) God help us all. "Mr. Sharon is over 200—resist." (Not true.) Uh-oh. "Mr. Sharon is over 175." (True.) "180." (True.) "185." (True.) "190." (Not true.) Ooh. Wow.

So, that's a little bit of a reversal over what it used to be. I think Sharon used to be high and came down, and Arafat was really down and has come up: "That's a fact." (True.) Okay. "Sharon was once higher—resist." (True.) "And now's come down—resist." (True.) "And Arafat was once lower and has now come up—resist." (True.) Yeah, you've got an oddball crisscross there, in which one has come down in order to win, and the other one is coming up in order to survive. I think Arafat realizes unless he re-owns integrity, he's a dead duck. And I think he realizes that it's not Palestine or himself, his political self that's at risk, it's integrity itself. I think it's intuitively dawning on him that unless he re-owns the power of integrity, he's a goner: "That's a fact—resist." (True.) Yeah, by God, he's getting it, hmm. So, all the people praying for it, it's working. Somebody's hearing it, you know. The first one that really regains integrity is going to win and win the respect of the world and the backing of the world. Whichever one finally comes out with integrity, is going to win. Okay. So, that's Arafat and Sharon.

Yogananda, we've calibrated him before, at 550. He would therefore be the perfect spiritual teacher. Let's say, all spiritual teachers are good for wherever you're at, see. If this guy tells you it's wrong to chop up infidels, that's a major advance, so he's a very good guru until there, you understand what I'm saying? [Level] 550 is the classical guru in our world. These are people that are unconditionally loving. What did we say he was, 550, yeah.

550. [Level] 540 is Unconditional Love. Anything that runs 540 and up is certainly worthy of great respect and, as we've said, the Twelve Step groups are 540. They represent the pure essence of spirituality. That which has no opinion on external issues tells you right away that it's not corruptible. There's no opinions on outside issues. Anything that has no opinions on outside issues can't be bought or sold, can it? Because there's no lever out there to grab them by. They don't care what you think of them; they don't need your vote; they don't need your money. They can just be who they are.

As I've said before, sometimes there's a disparity between the writings of a teacher and their current calibration. It's because as you evolve—don't forget a test of that comes up all the time, and you can buy its opposite. The power over others, I can remember being presented with that one, and I forget what that level was. We calibrated it later, but it was really infinite—I mean, enormous—power, unlimited by any limitation. And it was offered. All you had to do was say yes to it. In the book I'm finishing now, I feel responsible as a spiritual educator, teacher, whatever you want to call it, to forewarn people that as you go up, that which is Luciferic is waiting for you. It's waiting for you, and when you get there, then it heads for you. It's like the media doesn't bite you until you become a celebrity, you know what I mean. You're not influencing enough people, so when you start getting up there, now the sniper's bullet starts getting aimed at you. So, I feel it's a responsibility to educate the student about that; that as you evolve, that which would deny the reality of what you have realized as truth becomes challenged. And it's done cleverly. I think I wrote it rather specifically in the book I'm finishing now. I remember it at about 850 or so, coming in the realization out of nowhere; it's not via a person. No spiritual truth comes from other beings. You don't know what you know because "that told me," or some spirit-ascended spiritual master told you that. It's a realization of that which you are, so then, suddenly in the purity of that incredible space, comes the knowingness. It comes out of like a non-verbal realization; "Now that you are beyond personal karma, and there is no arbitrary God

to punish you, inasmuch as there is no payment and no consequences to anything you do, think, or say, you are free to have
absolute power over others." And that is the ultimate Luciferic.
And of course, that's the one that's apparently brought down a
number of teachers.

The other defect that the Luciferic offers on the way up is,
umm, to see Love as a trap. I remember that because that's a very
specific one, that as you go up higher and higher, the Luciferic will
come to you, either in the form of a person, a teacher, or an entity
coming through somebody you're talking to. They will say, "Don't
you see that love is just a trap?" And they will sometimes use the
Buddha's description of the ultimate reality as Void to verify it and
back it up. No, it's not Love that's a limitation to the realization of
the Infinite Reality—it's the attachment to it. None of these things
have any power within themself. All the things we're scared about
and taught about through all spiritual and religious instruction—
it isn't the thing itself, it's our attachment to it.

Is money and sex a great limitation to spiritual evolution? Well,
Ramakrishna said so—in young men, it's such a problem that he
forbid it. You weren't even allowed to touch money. Money and
sex were the two traps. Within a certain limited context, that's
so. In a broader context, no—it's the attachment to them. A free
being can go to the casino, win or lose and walk away, untouched,
huh. Untouched, because the reality is not involved in it. No, it's
the attachment to love and money. It's the attachment to power.
So, I saw the Luciferic. What the Luciferic is, is the temptation to
own the power of God, but not the love of God. You see? Because
the love of God, that which is divinity is both power and love.
If you negate the reality of the love, then you have nothing but
power over others.

The next question to the Luciferic, they haven't tried it since
because that would be disaster-ful. The next stake to the Luciferic
is, "What is your attachment to power, buddy?" Now that you
have no karmic consequences to pay, now that there's no arbitrary
God waiting up there from the Old Testament to beat the chocks
off of you, why don't you just do whatever you're going to do, forget about conscience—there's no payment can be extracted by

anyone. "All power is yours," that's what it says. Jesus got the same deal in the Garden of Gethsemane. Jesus got the same presentation, didn't he? "Kneel down and worship me, all power will be yours." So, the answer to that Luciferic demon—because you'll get them—if you're moving toward enlightenment, it'll be waiting for you. And teachers have failed to prepare their students with what the answer is. To the naïve mind, it sounds very convincing. It comes from a very high-feeling authority, this amazing realization and you have no consequences. There's nothing and no one to be answerable to, for. You're beyond human karma. "All power is yours." All power is yours. And if you stop at that point, you become a prince in the Luciferic realm.

And the question for that demon is this: "Of what good is your power? Of what use? Are you still attached to power? What do you want with power?" I remember one time somebody hated me very intensely, which I picked up on the inner. It was reported via dreams of somebody else, that this entity hated me. And this was when I was a celebrity in a different realm, you know, in New York. I had the biggest practice in the world—in the country and all. This guy hated me and I said, "What does he hate me for?" He envies your power. I said, "Power? What power?" I treat lots and lots of sick people. What is he talking about? A projection from his own unconscious, I guess. Because if you contextualize things in terms of power, then you see that as power. If a million people go, "Ohm, ohm, ohm," does that give you power? It doesn't change who you are, one iota.

We were talking about women before. The magnificence of the woman is the divinity within her womanhood. It's not her womanhood, per se, but the divinity expressing itself in this particular case as femininity; and when we get to Father's Day, expressing itself as masculinity. You see, those are just the world of form—it's only how it looks from a viewpoint of perception, viewpoint of perception. And as consciousness evolves, it transcends gender. You know that which you are has no limitation such as gender anyway.

All right. You've already got the answer to the ultimate, the one is the challenge to love—to sacrifice love for gain and power over others, and manipulation, sexual satisfaction or whatever. The other great temptation is the Luciferic. The teaching that love is an attachment and a limitation and a block to enlightenment is a major error: "We have permission to ask that—resist." (True.) "That is a statement of fact—resist." (True.) That is a statement of fact. And you see, the authority background of it is the misinterpretation of the Buddhic teaching of the ultimate Reality as void. Void is nothingness. What the Buddha meant was "no thingness," nothingness, beyond form. What the Buddha said was, "The Ultimate Truth is the Unmanifest, beyond form." "Resist." (True.) Beyond form. That's different. If the void was the absolute Reality, there would be nobody to tell you about it, wouldn't there? First of all, they'd have nothing to say and there would be no one there to say it. The ego will create a feeling of oblivion and you go into oblivion and because oblivion is not the same as the ultimate Reality, you can't stay there. And you come out of oblivion and you find yourself, three years old in a little cart, shocked to discover that you have a body again.

People ask me about the various religions in the world. So far, the Buddhists have maintained the strictest truth. The Buddhists have maintained the highest teaching. People have asked, "What's the highest teaching?" I think classic Buddhism: "The highest teaching is classic Buddhism—resist." (True.) Yeah, classic Buddhism is pretty much—it hasn't sold out for political gain, control, political power. See, what happened with Christianity, it got sold out piecemeal, doled out to the various rulers and emperors and various things. So far, Buddhism has avoided that. I don't know where Hinduism is currently.

Let's just see where the world is at, currently. Well, of course, you have to be quite definite in how you express this: "Current Protestantism as it is practiced in America—Protestantism, as a general, is over 485." (True.) "490." (True.) "495." (True.) "500." (True.) "505." (Not true.) Protestantism, 505, as of today. "Protestantism, the consciousness level of it is falling—resist." (True.) "Rising—resist." (Not true.) "It's becoming secularized." (True.) Oh, I see, it's being destroyed by secularization, yeah. All right. So, what happens is, as a religion gets *older*, as it begins to get secularized by the civilization in which it finds itself. You know, financial considerations—it takes money to build churches, and you've got to build a congregation, and everything costs money.

So, of the world's current religions, let's say, let's ask for: "We can ask about Hinduism—resist." (True.) "Hinduism, as practiced in its most pristine level in India, currently is over 500—resist." (True.) "560." (True.) "580." (Not true.) "575." (True.) "580." (Not true.) Hinduism at its best in current India comes out at 575. Islam: "Islam, as currently practiced in the Arabic world, calibrates over 200—resist." (Not true.) No. Islam has just been destroyed.

Christianity, Catholicism. Okay: "Catholicism in the current world, exclusive of priestly events, is over 500." (True.) "510." (Not true.) "Catholicism at its best, at its pristine best, in current America is over 510—resist." (Not true.) "It's over 509—resist." (Not true.) "It's over 505." (True.) "506." (Not true.) It's loving. It's loving, but it has lost its pristine—don't forget, in the beginning, it was 1,000. At the time of Christ, Christianity was 1,000, so it has come down considerably. Islam has come down considerably. Hinduism still maintains its—what did we say—575. That's very high, 575. And, that's close to Enlightenment at 600. Wow.

And Buddhism has declined the least. Let's see what Buddhism is at currently: "The vehicle Hinayana—we have permission to ask about Hinayana." (True.) "Hinayana calibrates over 800 to 850." (Not true.) "Hinayana Buddhism calibrates over 850." (True.) "860." (True.) "870." (Not true.) We got 870. Somebody put that down. "Mahayana, which includes Zen, calibrates over 850." (True.) "860." (True.) "865." (Not true.) Did we get 860 for both of them? Let's do it again: "Hinayana and Mahayana are almost identical, as far as calibrated level of consciousness—resist." (True.) They're almost identical. One is the lesser vehicle; one is the greater vehicle.

Lotus Land Buddhism is something else. Let's do Lotus Land. Lotus Land is closest to Christianity: "We have permission to do Lotus Land—resist." (True.) "It's over 550." (True.) "580." (True.) "590" (True.) "600." (Not true.) "Lotus Land is right at 600—resist." (True.) Yeah, I would suspect so. Lotus Land is right at 600. Lotus

Land is the Buddha of salvation, in which the Buddha becomes the Savior. It's the equivalent of Christianity. The radical, the spiritual realist, you might say. The spiritual teachers been kicked around throughout the centuries realizes in this world which calibrated less than 190 over the many centuries, that the best you could hope for was to reach Unconditional Love. Don't forget, in a world that's dominated by hatred, love—I mean, hatred, anger, starvation, war, killing, rape, suicide—500 is almost astronomical. So, in a way, Jesus Christ, and the Lotus Land Buddhist, the Buddha of Salvation, the Great Saviors are saying, "Aim for 500 or 540, and from there on, you don't have to worry." Let's see if that's true: "You get to 540, you won't have to worry—resist." (True.)

I calibrated the Native American. So, the Native American, you see, was into monotheism. Of course, we don't know how far back their history is or what their teachings were back that far. Ancient Egypt, we still have, you know, actually the writings from those days. But the Native American believed in the Great Spirit of authority, a monotheist. Actually was a monotheist. I think we calibrated Chief Detroit, who was very famous. The "Recitations of Chief Detroit" are quite profound. All right: "Chief Detroit, who was an Iroquois, calibrated over 700—resist." (True.) "710." (True.) "720." (True.) "730." (Not true.) [Level] 730. That's higher than Mohammad. Mohammad came in at 731. So that capacity to realize the presence of an infinite Oneness. The infinite divinity out of which all of creation manifests. See, the Native American could see the expression of divinity in all things that live—brother elk, brother rabbit—apologizing to the fact, "I've got to knock you out of body." See, the animal doesn't die when you knock it out of body. It's just knocked out of body: "That's a fact—resist." (True.) Yeah. Sometimes the animal hardly even notices it: "The animal doesn't really notice it most of the time—resist." (True.) Yeah, it doesn't notice it most of the time—flying around in a little fly's body—swat! Now it's flying around in its little etheric body. It doesn't even really notice. It comes back into another and it's flying and it's got amnesia for that—it doesn't remember that it "was" and then "wasn't." Doesn't worry about not "being," because it doesn't remember that it wasn't! So, the Native American already knew that the animal doesn't actually die. It sacrifices this physical manifestation. Now it has to go on the other side and wait to come back again. And so, "Thank you brother, for giving up your physicality for the maintenance of my physicality; and don't take this personally, but I gotta eat you."

All right. So, the intellect puts that down as—what is it? Pantheism, and Catholicism, it's an error to see divinity in all of nature and in all that exists, because traditional religion tends to be seeing God as transcendent. You see, probably the reason Buddhism comes up so high is because the Buddha taught that realization of the absolute truth, by whatever you call it—divinity, or the Ultimate, no reality. You call it the Buddha nature is to merely realize that which we talked about earlier—that which you really are that instant right before the mind gets in and interrupts the awareness of who you are. So, the Buddha said God is Immanent. So, the Ultimate Divinity is both Immanent within, as the Self with a capital S, and Transcendent, as the Supreme. When Krishna writes of the Supreme, it's really meant to be not only the Supreme Transcendent, but the Supreme Immanent as the Self, as the essence of That Which You Are.

So, the Native American, then, was quite evolved. And happily, he didn't know he was evolved, or he would have made a thing out of it. Chopped it to pieces, know what I'm saying?

* * *

Addiction is a whole story in itself. I did probably one of the first lectures on consciousness—it was on addiction, back in the early '80s. I did it in California at a conference on Consciousness and Addiction. My understanding of addiction at that time was, is that, see, all this stuff from here down [low on MoC] is painful. Painful as compared to its not being there. Drugs block out your experiencing of all this here [low on MoC]. A drug itself only calibrates around 75 or 80: "Alcohol calibrates around 75." (True.) "Drugs calibrate around 75 to 80." (True.) See, as chemicals, these chemicals just calibrate around 75 or 80. The awareness of the presence of God within is blocked by the conversation and the energy fields of the ego. It's like the clouds in the sky block off the radiance of the sun. What the drugs do is silence these energy fields [low on MoC]—anesthetize them; therefore, you only feel the radiance of the higher vibrations. Now, all of these vibrations are going on at once. Let's say, light comes through a spectrum, this is "Who I Am," huh? The experience, even if experienced *once*, is like a near-death experience. The first time you get high, you already *got* it. The first time you feel that lovely, gorgeous, "I love everybody," "isn't life grand?" Whoa! You've got it right now. Right at that moment. Anybody who doesn't keep repeating that must be stupid say, "I'm going to back to here [low on MoC], and go back to the office and be p.o.'d at my boss, and worry about my work. What's the matter with that idiot? Why doesn't he just block it off and stay there? Stay stoned and live there, you know what I'm saying?" That's what the voice within says. Why should I live this miserable, horrible life? Have a few beers on the way to work. It's not hurting anybody; it's my money, right? Well, so that euphoria, then, is not—the drug doesn't have the capacity to create a high.

The point is, it is not the drug that creates this feeling of euphoria: "The feeling of euphoria is the radiance of the Self—resist." (True.) So, if we block off negative energies, what's left is the radiance of the Self. You feel high, you feel fantastic, you feel great. The only problem is, you didn't really transcend the lower sense of the ego; you only temporarily blocked it off. You found a shortcut. Somehow that creates some kind of a karmic debt, kind of a karmic debt, right? "Somehow that creates some kind of a karmic debt—resist." (True.) Yeah. Somehow, it's as though the money that you stole, you now owe back later, with interest. Anybody who's gone through withdrawal from drugs or alcohol knows what I mean. You pay it, and with interest. All that you stole, you might say, in an artificial manner, now you're not allowed to touch it. If you're going to recover, one day at a time, you can't touch any of it. So, then what happens is the way back legitimately is discovered.

So, the Twelve Steps is nothing but how to come from an artificially induced euphoria back into a lovingness which you have actually become. Now, because you have become it, you own it. It's no longer vulnerable. Nobody can take it away from you because lovingness is a condition; it's a way of being. It's a way of being, and as members of this group know, because there's a great deal of lovingness here. As you walk through Walmart, your lovingness goes with you and people intuit it. That's why they smile at you, and they're open and very vulnerable with you. You see, what love is, is an openness and a vulnerability. A lady, I bumped into her basket and she was just wide open, totally vulnerable to me. You know, I could have snatched her purse and run. She probably would have said, "Thank you. How can we help you? Would you like another purse?"

Trust. Part of love is trust. The more loving we are, the more capable we are of trust. That's the way we get out of the negative. So, that's the story on addiction, pretty much. You get addicted—what you're addicted to is this state [high on MoC]. Once you experience this state, nothing less than that is going to ever do, I'll tell you. Near-death experience. Nothing, nothing in this world comes near it. The longing to return to that state of awareness, that condition, that presence hangs with you, and that's what the addict has to get off of, and that's why recovery is slow, difficult, and statistically, uh. . . . These levels are not necessarily progressive. You know, it's not like grade school, and then third grade, fourth grade. You can make great leaps. Hitting bottom, the story of addiction is. . . . To me, addiction is the fast way to God. You either die, or you get it. You either die, or you get it, so it's like last-gaspers, you know. You've been 63 times on this planet, and you're getting pretty desperate. Ah, the fastest way, it either makes you or breaks you, is addiction. You either die of insanity, agony, and a horrible death, or you transcend it. So, you can go all the way from down here [low on MoC], suicidal, and suddenly go into a presence, infinite state, incredible state—incredible state, like the presence of God. From the depths of hell, one can call forth, "If there is a God, I ask him to help me." Then remember nothing, and suddenly stand in the infinite presence.

It was the Ultimate. From the depths of hell to the presence of the Infinite. So, can you jump levels? You bet you can. As we said, you can go from Grief, stop seeing it as loss, feeling sorry for yourself and juicing it out of self-pity, and seeing it as freedom. Where's Freedom up here [on MoC], 200 and something.

* * *

The date of death, we've said before, is already set at the time of birth, the date is already set: "Is that date like equivalent of written in cement—resist." (True.) "Do we have other options—resist." (Not true.) No, you don't, really. Oh, you think you did. All right. I don't have to feel bad about that one anymore now. I had the opportunity and didn't take it. And for years after, I said, "God, what an idiot you were, man, you had—there you were in that infinite Presence, one with the infinite Lovingness of the universe, and you said, 'I'm going back in the body.'" What a stupid idiot.

To see the divinity within all that exists. Well, the divinity… the existence of divinity within certain aspects of life, or certain gurus, pieces of consciousness that speaks to you, et cetera, it's just that they're more recognizable, you see. That same divinity is within all that exists. It is not possible for anything to exist unless it comes out of Creation. All that comes out of Creation, then, has within it the essence of divinity, or it could not "be," anything could "be," huh?

We saw that Buddhism had declined the least of all the world's religions, very interestingly, because it stuck to its own spirituality rather than getting involved in local politics. What happened to most religions, I think, is that they got invaded by the local politics. To get the church to align itself with this regime, versus the House of Hapsburg versus the House of Something or other. Of course, it's what cost it a lot of its believability. So, I think we've answered most of the questions that we had on top of the list. I want to make sure.

We're often asked about Joel Goldsmith and we've done him many times. You see, there's many spiritual teachers that are in the high 400s: "Joel Goldsmith is in the high 400s." (True.) "490." (True.) "495." (True.) "Joel Goldsmith's writings are over 495." (True.) "His writings are over 500." (Not true.) "His writings are about 495—resist." (True.) Okay. He's taking you as far as the intellect can take you in the understanding of truth. The teachers in the high 400s are often very excellent because they have mastered the knowledge, and of course, spiritual searchers are very often in the 400s, and the erudition that comes in the high 400s is what springs you into the 500s. How do you get out of the 400s? Because you learn within the 400s, the world of the intellect, that the intellect is not going to give you the answer. So, the greatest fruit that the intellect can give you is, "I ain't what you're looking for." Whoa. Because all of society thinks all you've got to do is read another book and take another course and you'll get there.

Nisargadatta Maharaj's level of consciousness on the earth was over 700. The book, *I Am That*, I think, is 700. Other books, really, are in the high 400s.

Somebody asked me what love is. Well, okay. As commonly understood, love is an emotion, and this emotion goes from "here" to "there." Love is something you give; love is something you can get. Consequently, love is something you can lose. Therefore, love is volitional, it's conditional. Love is also something that's deserved. You have to earn love; you have to pay for love. It's like a commodity, a very pleasant one and highly regarded, but it's losable. It goes from here to there, and therefore it's subject to dissolution and vulnerable to attack. It's something that people fear the loss of, et cetera.

What Is Love, Actually?

So, what is love, actually? Well, those you who've gone into really high spaces know that love—the love we're talking about, is really about up here [high on MoC]. Love is a way of being. It's a way of being with the world. The condition of lovingness prevails as a permanency because it's what you are. It's what you've become. The willingness to be friendly in Walmart is because you're a loving being—it's coming from your lovingness. It doesn't depend on whether this lady with her basket smiles at you or appreciates it; it's just who you are. And it's who you are in all times, places, and conditions. It doesn't change. It's not given, and it's not lost. It's not taken away. It's not something you earn—it's what you've become, similar to generosity.

Generosity is a way of being in the world. It doesn't have to do with money. Generosity has to do with the willingness to be open and share what you are with life, for . . . what? For the good of life itself. Only because of that's what you are. It's because that's the way you've become. You automatically appreciate life in all its expressions. You know what I mean? You drive along a country road, and there's a bunch of cows, you know. A bunch of cattle there, and you can't help but stop and love 'em. The cow's life expressing itself in that beautiful way that a cow is, you know, a cow's just a beautiful creature being what it is, you know what I'm saying? And there's the little calves there, being what they are.

We've said that evolution, as it appears in physicality, is the reflection of that which has occurred on the level of consciousness. It's on the level of consciousness that form evolves into the forms that we see as life on earth. The form can then be optionally energized by energies on the other side, you might say—we'll just say for ease of speech—"on the other side," can opt to be the life energy within that form. That form has a central—you remember in *Power vs. Force*, we talked about attractor fields. In the nonlinear domain of what appears as chaos, what appears as chaos, multiple orange kitties all over the planet, there's a central attractor field of orange kitty-ness. We could even draw it if we had a computer.

Nature draws attractor fields for you all the time. All you have to do is fly in a plane and look at the formation of the earth below you, and the education. There's a beautiful series of videos on right now on TV called *The Blue Planet*. Anyway, incredible beauty, incredible beauty at the depths of the sea. Stunning creatures. So stunningly beautiful, you just suck in your breath—you go, "That's existing, 5,000 feet down in the dark?" Whoo. Gorgeous, radiant, beautiful. But you see the schools of fish, wheeling as though they are one. You see the whole tens of thousands of fish, all in a design like this. You see the same thing with the birds taking off. They all go like this. Well, the presumption of the ego, which believes in causality, is that this bird is flying like a squadron of fighters, this many feet from this one. It thinks that these birds are following this bird, and causing these. . . . Actually, what's happening, these birds are not following each other at all. These birds are being controlled by an attractor field in the invisible domain. Each bird is uniquely controlled by the same attractor field, and that's why they line up. They're not following each other at all. So, when you see the birds whirling like that, that's the demonstration of the attractor field which is in the invisible domain becoming manifest in a flock of birds in flight. You see five million minnows all turning as one and the shine of light as they swing. They swing like one, one being in thousands and thousands of bodies, simultaneously. That's the attractor field.

The animal gods of the Native Americans, the many gods of the Hindu pantheon all represent to me the attractor fields. In other words, there is central to all orange kitty-ness, the essence of all that makes orange kitty-ness and it radiates out what looks to perception as individual, separate orange kitties, but there's only one orange kitty-ness radiating out. Do you understand what I'm saying?

So, the essence of each genus and species then, exists on the invisible domain and actualizes within the physical: "What I said is true—resist." (True.) "There is one orange kitty—resist." (True.) There is one orange kitty. The reason I know this is I've had a whole series of orange kitties and it's always the same kitty. I mean, an orange kitty's nature is the same. You ever notice that? Doberman Pinschers, they're all the same, you know. So, we love each species and genus because it represents in physicality, certain characteristics that we've come to love and appreciate.

"In the condition of the human, we have individual karma—resist." (True.) So, we don't represent a group—the manifestation of—otherwise there would be like one human being and we would all radiate out the sameness, the sameness. But what we radiate mainly is difference, right? There's a sameness to our essence, but a difference: "Perhaps different races represent sort of a coalition of energies—resist." (Not true.) No, they don't either. So. "Human-ness is an individual karma—resist." (True.) "Orange kitty-ness is a group karma—resist." (True.) So that's in certain spiritual teach-ings, that animals share a group karma, whereas mankind has individual karma. So, orange kitties then have a group orange kitty-ness karma. They have pretty good karma.

"Humans have the capacity to reincarnate in sub-human forms—resist." (Not true.) No, I've asked that before. We always get no. So, you don't have to worry about coming back as a frog. Only a frog gets to come back as a frog. All right.

Well, is the highest level of enlightenment better to help oth-ers become enlightened? You might say so, but that again is a pro-gram that is projected on the condition. The condition only is what it is. It is what it is to the world because . . . because it *is* that. It's similar to the question about loving, lovingness. You're not loving "in order to" anything. You understand what I'm saying? Once a person becomes loving, there's no purpose to that loving-ness. It's just what they are. They become that. So, that lovingness doesn't like, present itself in Walmart in order to make other shop-pers happy, or for any other reason. It's just who you are. And who you are turns some people on and probably makes other people hate you. Lots of people hate love. There are countries in the world in which it was illegal, you know. Cambodia was one of them— remember Pol Pot? You were put to death if you displayed affec-tion and lovingness in public. Made it suitable for execution. The Japanese warrior in Nanking who showed lovingness toward his captive, I'm sure would . . . may have gotten himself bayoneted on the spot, for insubordination.

"Is there a correlation between intelligence and conscious-ness?" I never asked that before: "There is some meaningful cor-relation between I.Q. and consciousness—resist." (Not true.) No. You can have an I.Q. and be very stupid. You can be very stupid and be very beneficial to the world, you know. So, apparently not. It's just that some people are built more muscular. Somebody came up today and to me he was the perfect mesomorph, you know what I mean? He had like muscles and bone.

I was born an ectomorph, you know. Lifting anything over 50 pounds has always been a struggle my whole life. I always tell people—people are born somatotypes: endomorph, mesomorph, and ectomorph. An endomorph tends to be chunky, tends to be very family-oriented, got to have family around you. Values family-ness, home-ness, and domesticity. And dieting probably isn't going to do any good at all. If you look at a candy bar, you gain half a pound. They have a wonderful digestive tract.

The mesomorph tends to be more muscular and capable of sports. And the mesomorph, as they get older, if they sit in front of the TV and drink beer, they're gonna put it on. But if the meso-morph cuts down their diet and exercises, they will lose weight. So, the mesomorph can either gain or lose weight. Endomorph is going to stay on diet pills, but they aren't going to really take much weight off. Not going to change your lifestyle anyway.

The ectomorph is skinny and neurotic. Thin and wiry, and somewhat nervous and neurotic, and prone to nervous break-downs and never gonna gain weight and eating too much just makes them throw up, doesn't gain weight.

So, we sort of accept our fate, you might say. If you're an endo-morph, quit struggling with it. Become the happy, jolly, fat person that everybody loves. If you're a mesomorph, be sure and diet and exercise if you gain weight. And if you're an ectomorph, you're too neurotic to worry about it anyway, so . . .

Now, you can't rate anything up and down the scale [MoC]. You can only know where it is. Many of the world's best spiritual teachers are in the high 400s. They are more capable of express-ing, verbalizing, making comprehensible and understandable the spiritual truths than people who are in the 800s, let's say. Most people in the 800s are totally unintelligible. Most of them stay home. You never meet them in public. First of all, there's noth-ing to say. That's quite a roadblock, to begin with. Take you 20,

30 years to figure what you're going to say about all this. There's nothing to say about it. Most spiritual teachers of a very advanced enlightenment are not necessarily good teachers, any more than Ignacy Paderewski was a great piano teacher. Vaslav Nijinsky was probably a very lousy ballet teacher, you know what I'm saying? The fact that you're a great musician doesn't make you a great teacher. The best teachers or good musicians are themselves not genius musicians; otherwise, they'd be on the road. In childhood, artistic merit was greatly appreciated by the family. We traveled endless miles to see Nijinsky or any great performers of the day. And my grandfather on my mother's side knew a lot of them personally. Many of them were great virtuosos, but as teachers, forget it—make one mistake, "Get out of here, I can't stand it, you stupid idiot!"

So, a great teacher very often, the high 400s, these are often the most erudite teachers. They're the most erudite teachers. They can compare the world's literature, cite all the references that reinforce and confirm each other. So, they are great clarifiers of spiritual truth. So, you can't say that a teacher at 540 is better than a teacher at 480. They're different; they're teaching different things. The higher one goes up the scale, the more it is that the presence of that which you are, itself has the transformative effect, rather than verbatim, the wording, yeah, the wording. So, there are some beings in whose presence one feels an elevation of consciousness, but they may not write at all. They don't have any linguistic verbal fluency. They are not great writers. And there's great writers who have the data down pat. They're interesting, but you don't exactly go into a state of samadhi in their presence, eh. So, one is not better than the other. They serve different purposes.

Very often, when you go with the way of the heart, which we will talk more about at a later date, you can bypass and shoot all the way up, because love bypasses the intellect altogether. You understand? Love takes you to 500, and it's beyond reason. Someone will say, "Why do you love that person, thing?" You can't give any reason why. Can't give any reason. Certain music, you instantly transcend: "The music I'm thinking of now calibrates over 500." (True.) "520." (True.) "530" (True.) "540." (True.) "550." (True.) "560." (True.) "570." (Not true.) My God, he's way up there. Andrea Bocelli. So, you see what the space that you go into as you listen to that music, if the pathway of the heart is open in you, tends to bring tears. That's why it's not good to drive to! It's bad music to drive to, because you lose all interest in going anywhere for anything about anything. I mean, everything is total and complete right now. Where is there to go for what? You know what I mean.

So, I think that, that which is of great beauty, the great cathedrals of the world you know, calibrate right around 700, Chartres, you go into a cathedral like Chartres, and you can't stop crying; it's just overwhelming. The great cathedrals I've been in, they just overwhelm you. All thoughts stop; the joy of beauty comes up and you can't function in that state. I've noticed there's no graffiti in the great cathedrals of the world, isn't that interesting?

Because that which hates beauty is the source of graffiti. Graffiti usually desecrates that which is, what does it desecrate? It usually desecrates that which is below 200. At 500, even the weirdest person doesn't have what it takes. So great beauty then, overwhelms people, sets them back into the reality of the Self, out of which such thinkingness does not arise. The exception of extreme madness. The Pietà calibrates at over 550, 580, 590? The Pietà calibrates at 590. That which desecrated the Pietà, its level was over 60.

That which is of incredible beauty has the tendency to throw you back into the Self. You can walk into the world's great cathedrals that have been there for a thousand years; incredible music, incense, and beauty shine forth through the stained glass windows; it's not your religion, but the reverence, the collective reverence, the worship of God expressing itself as this incredible beauty, has an uplifting experience. One then ascribes that experience through the out-thereness of the cathedral. No, the cathedral gives you the experience of that which is always present at all times within yourself, but you only allow yourself this experience under these conditions. That which you are experiencing is the presence of the Divine within. Incredible beauty, then, unleashes the dam in which that which is love, that which is sacred, shines forth, and that radiance is what makes you feel like crying. That incredible beauty brings a lump to your throat. Incredible beauty as it rises makes the hair on the back of your head stand up and then as it gets even higher, you can't stop crying. Is that so?

Those of you who have gone into incredibly beautiful spaces know that you can't stop crying at a certain level. At a certain level, you can't even witness anything that has to do with love. It just breaks you up. A little puppy walking down the street, you break out in tears. I mean, it's adorable, its lovableness and you can see what it means to the owner, you know, the whole space of all that lovingness is just too much; it just knocks you out. So, there's a difficult time there, a difficult time of weeping and crying over the presence of divinity as beauty and love.

Q: *"Is consciousness a byproduct of spirit entering dense matter?"*

No, no it's not. Consciousness arises prior to matter. Genesis is pretty correct, according to our own research, that out of what appeared as chaos to perception, which is really non-form, arose life as consciousness. The power of consciousness is such that it can initiate life when it touches matter, and that matter then evolves from below up. So, creation is from above down, and then we see the evolution of life forms from the bottom up. From the ooze, to "Us-ens." Then we can look down on the worm. We'll get somebody to look down on.

What is the difference between mind and consciousness? Consciousness is the field which supports the phenomena called "mind." Consciousness itself is without form, without form. Just before you think a thought, what you're experiencing is awareness, which is an aspect of consciousness. If you want to, you can watch and see right before every thought, you have an opportunity. The opportunity presents itself continuously. It lasts about 1/10,000th of a second. You've got to be quick, eh? "That space is

1/10,000th of a second, approximately—resist." (True.) "It's more than that—resist." (Not true.) No, it's not more than that. Darn it! It's always been right at 1/10,000th of a second. When we say that, it sounds very, very minimal, and who the heck's gonna make it through the crack in 1/10,000th of a second? That's in only temporal, physical time, and that doesn't sound like much. But in that space of that 1/10,000th of a second, you're looking at eternity, which is outside of time, so you have a window open to that which is beyond time—the infinite. One-ten thousandth of a second, what does that mean? What does that mean? It means, then, you become aware of your thoughts as sort of a thingness thing. It's sort of like your thought is a thing. Right prior to this thing occupying the space of your attention, is a space. If there wasn't an empty space, the thought would have no place to present itself. You know what I'm saying? Without a blank screen, there is nothing for a thought to project itself upon. With a little self-reflection, the best place to become enlightened is driving, riding in a taxicab, any place, waiting in the line at the supermarket. One's thoughts go by nonchalantly, and suddenly one sees one instant right before the thought, that's who you are. And you pull back into that no-thinkingness prior to thought. It's there all the time. It's there all the time. So, it's said that the entryway into enlightenment is in the instant of "now." That "now" is always present. It only takes a curiosity, really. You don't have to fast and join a monastery or a nunnery, beat drums and gongs and chant all day, and beat yourself, deprive yourself. Every possible instant of now is forever present. Outside of time, forever is this moment. So, you really, in a way, have forever to notice this. Out of sheer curiosity—forget about enlightenment, forget about God, all that. Just out of sheer curiosity, watch and see that each thought arises in an empty space. Be with the empty space, and as the next thought arises, the empty space is there again. The empty space presents itself continuously, and then one sees, "I'm the space and not the thought." It's simple, huh?

Q: *"If everything is perfect, what's the point of perfecting anything, because it is perfect already?"*

Everything is perfect as it is. What does that mean? Nothing can be other than the perfection of that which it is. That has to do with a thing that's very hard to explain. The radical identity of self of that which it is with that which it is, in which there is no absence of information that has to be projected onto it by the observer. What you're asking is easy to see, but difficult to answer in a verbal form. To formulize a piece of plastic, it's absolutely perfect. It's perfectly, it's perfectly, exactly that which it is. [Bends and picks up a tiny piece of plastic from the stage floor.] The perfection is that in that it fulfills its karmic destiny at all times, absolutely. If it has no destiny, it could be a camel, an imperfect camel.

But it's not an imperfect piece of plastic. It would be imperfect in the eye of the groundskeeper, who feels it should be swept away, huh. But that's trying to impose form on what is. What it is, is the absolute perfect expression of all that it takes throughout the evolution of all of time, through the invention of plastic, through the "all of us being here," through the gravity, through the barometric pressure, for this building to be here, for Sedona to be founded, et cetera. It took all of that for this divine piece of plastic to be where it is.

So, perfection is then what you see it as. There are different levels of perfection, because there are really a lot of definitions, you see. In the absolute, the word *perfection* would be meaningless. Just like the word *beauty* is meaningless when you stand there looking at a sunset, *incredible*. All words you could use would be irrelevant, hmm. Everything is perfectly what it is at every moment because there is no other possibility. Any other possibility is an intellectual positionality—it does not reflect any reality.

Nothing can be anything except that which it is. To be that which it is, it already has to be perfectly that which it is, or it couldn't exist at all. For the evolution of consciousness to take the forms that it takes. So, as consciousness evolves, it takes these forms. Here's Neanderthal man. It gets to "here" from "there."

So, you can't make it wrong for being in the process of getting "here"—it isn't here yet. That which was what it was, as evolution became more and more conscious, *Homo spiritus* is just born—five minutes ago! *Homo spiritus* is just barely the latest evolutionary tree of mankind. It doesn't value the physical and the material anymore; it doesn't value wealth; it doesn't value. The ego comes out of the evolution of animal consciousness and survival.

Homo spiritus doesn't even value that anymore. You can give me 10 million dollars to do something non-integrous and it would sound like a joke. Wouldn't it? You'd sell your soul for what? Don't be ridiculous. To someone who's not at that level, it would be a major temptation, you understand. So, we've become a different kind of an entity. If I say to you, visiting a relic will have a spiritual advantage, you'd say, "Hey, let's go." If it does not have a spiritual advantage, you wouldn't leave, would you? So, we are brought together by, by spiritual intention, that which sets our karma. So, we share a common karma. People dedicated to spiritual intention, that is what becomes paramount, surmounts other objectives.

—

CHAPTER 3

MEDITATION AND SPIRITUAL WORK

I was never very happy about this physicality, as I was saying; but suddenly at age three, out of oblivion there was the shock of this "this-ness." Aw, my God, it was awful. And so, we're all set to go? Out of happy oblivion, there was suddenly "this-ness." And "this-ness" has been like a plague ever since, to get beyond "this-ness." This physicality which people strangely become enamored of. I don't know, they seem like they suffer from some kind of insanity that they enjoy this thing, but with a great deal of endeavor, you can get it to be an enjoyable mechanism. And so, it's a big rag doll that I've been putting up with all these years.

This week I was 75, so for 72 years I've been putting up with this thing, which has certainly earned me the karma of getting rid of it someday. The good karma of getting rid of it someday. So, that's somewhat different than a lot of people look at the whole situation. But apparently that came out of some lifetimes as a Hinayana Buddhist, I was a very devout Buddhist monk, and the ultimate Reality was Voidness. And consequently, when I went out of body, I went into void and don't remember anything. Don't remember nuttin' till you come back in the next lifetime. But as you reach a certain level of awareness, you remember the previous lifetimes, and they all string together like, frankly, it's like this lifetime. It's all the same lifetime. But I was just looking at a couple of them yesterday because something came up about them, and you saw almost the flip-flop nature—one lifetime being "this" and creating all kinds of negative bad karma, then the next lifetime, flopping over to undo all that. I said, "Whoa, that was really very interesting how they tied together."

Well, today we're talking about meditation. But first we sort of start out by validating the reality in which we are here. In which everything is occurring of its own. You realize that nothing is causing anything else. That was the first lecture, to transcend the whole illusion of causality, because that is the whole structure of the ego. It sees everything as causing everything else and becomes entrapped by that. All the ego mechanisms are laid somehow on causality. Something out there is causing me to feel this way. We see ourselves as the victims of some mysterious force called "cause" instead of seeing ourselves as the context in which we witness all that. So, we start out the lectures by just recalling that nothing is causing anything else. Everything is occurring spontaneously as the fulfillment of the expression of its own essence from moment to moment.

So, if we're stuck in the word *cause*, then, we'll move up to cause, and then we'll move beyond cause; if we are going to stick with the word *cause*, then we see that there's only one cause for everything, and that cause is the cause of every instant. The cause of the hand being where it is, is the total action of the entire universe since the beginning of time manifesting itself via the will of God by Divine ordinance as creation, and out of creation arises the essence, and the essence out of the energy of creation, then expresses itself as the fulfillment of its essence. The cause of this instant is exactly the same as the cause of this instant, is exactly the same as the cause of this instant, and that is the totality of the entire universe since the beginning of all of time. So, that every instant is the fulfillment of the creative potential of God manifesting as the essence of that which this is fulfills the potentiality of its essence, which in the case of a hand is to move forward, seemingly in space. So, if we jump the presumption that there's something causing it to do that, then we see that with absolute freedom, the universe is merely like a flower being what it is.

You see the flower—this instant doesn't cause the flower to grow this instant, it doesn't *cause* the flower. The flower is unfolding its infinite potentiality of being a flower as the fulfillment of its Divine design. Nothing is causing it to do that. The sun doesn't cause it to do that. The rain doesn't cause it to do that. The seed doesn't cause it to do that. Putting it in your window in a pot doesn't cause the flower to do that. The flower is doing it of its own. It's fulfilling the destiny, the potential destiny, of its own essence. Consequently, at every second in which it is doing that is absolutely perfect. At this moment it's perfect, at this moment it's perfect because perfection is that it should do this, and because it is doing that, at every moment it is the perfect fulfillment of the will of God. Therefore, the entire universe stands in absolute perfection from instant to instant, right? Thank you, God, for saying that. I mean, I never could have said that. That was cool, man. But that is the way it is.

When you first see that, it lays you out. When you first walk into that and it reveals itself, if you can function for a few years—you can't function for some years, actually. Some years before one could function again. Because all is happening of its own. Well, the freedom that arises from that realization. How to arrive at that realization is what we're talking about today. We're talking about meditation, one of the great, time-honored traditions and ways to the awareness of the presence of God.

Now, meditation itself is an enormous subject. I'm sure we could fill this whole book with all the books written on meditation throughout the centuries. The great gurus, the great teachers of meditation, the meditation centers, the Buddhist traditions, yoga, the Indian, Aryan traditions, and in the Far East, of course, there's an enormous amount of literature and training.

Meditation need not be in the context of any particular religion or spiritual teaching. Friends of ours in Korea, Dr. Moon, has a meditation center, and you ask her, "Is it Christian?" "No." "Is it Buddhist?" "No." "Is it Hindu?" "No." "What is it?" "It's a meditation center," she says, and you get it. You just go there and meditate. Oh, wow. In other words, the process itself then unfolds to the inner layers of the ego; you'll transcend the ego. All right.

So, let's talk a little bit about the various techniques, many of which of course are well-established in the literature, have specific training programs. Many become very detailed in posture, diet, breathing. Many are accompanied by complicated breathing mechanisms. There are all kinds of incredible meditative techniques. We're not going to talk about them today because the world's literature is full of instructions, instruction centers, traditions, postures, breathing exercises, pranayama. We'll talk more about the essence of the meditative process itself, which is common to all of them. It's very neat to be able to shave your head, to leave the world, join a Zen monastery and sit zazen for 10 or 20 years. I love it! It pulls me. I have to resist it all the time. It's a natural state, and anything else, in a way, is sort of a drag.

I was the psychiatric consultant to the Zen monastery in New York. It was up in the little mountains right north of New York City. I forget where it is. Anyway, I used to go to the First Zen Institute in New York City. So, meditation itself, even, you know, as a lifestyle, is extremely attractive.

The average person is not able to do that, and consequently how can we obtain the benefits of meditation without going through formal renunciation?

So, what meditative awareness can we have, walking about and functioning within the ordinary world? And so, we'll talk about generally two styles of meditation, and we'll talk about ways to transcend the mind, so it'll be a busy morning—yes, come to think of it. Now that I've started to think again myself, I say, "Whoa, you got to go through all that. Yes. Yes, all that stuff there.

Well, let's start with a generality, that there is content and there is context. Context, you know, totally changes content. And a great deal of error arises in not being aware of the relationship of content and context. What we're looking for in meditation is how to transcend content and realize that the Self, that which we are, is the context, hmm? And how can we do that? There are two ways. One I call macular focus, which is central focus, intense fixity on the content of the ego, on the content of which you're looking at and doing; and the other is what I would call peripheral, peripheral vision. If we compare it to vision, the macula is that fovea in the back of the retina that focuses very specifically on details. If you look at a fly and then you focus on the eye of the fly, then you are being very specific and focusing on a very, very small, concentrated area. That's sort of macular vision. Then we have peripheral vision. Because, although I can see the content of what is in front of my eyes, there is a greater generality. A person who's interested in spiritual evolution learns to focus the sense of Self, the sense of awareness, the alertness, progressively more and more to the peripheral vision. One becomes quite peripheral in experiencing the world from moment to moment. One is aware of the general context. Now, the general context out of which the world seems to arise or appear, is silent and invisible. So, the ultimate context then is the silent invisibility, almost the space and silence out of which allows experience to be possible. If it is not for the background of silence, you cannot hear these words. If it is not for the emptiness of infinite, you might say, "no-thingness" of space, you would not be able to observe physicality. You couldn't see buildings or persons. To be aware at all times of the infinite space, the infinite potentiality, out of which this moment seems to be arising, is somewhat aligned with the awareness that all is happening of its own. That everything is spontaneously occurring without any intervention, without any causality. It's as though there is an infinite concert in which everything is happening spontaneously of its own, and one is the witness of what appears to be happening.

This can be done formally in seated meditation, and we'll get to that. We're trying to talk about how to reach a higher state of awareness even though one is functioning in the world. You begin to witness that everything is happening of its own, and that there is nothing causing it to be that way. So, as you transcend cause, you then become aware that everything is happening spontaneously. If we sit down to meditate, let's say we sit down to meditate, the problem is almost always the thinkingness of the mind.

So, we'll talk now more about the meditative process in a formal sense. You know, Ramana Maharshi always recommended that—he always said you don't have to join a monastery to become enlightened, that the householder can go about his business and all he has to do is keep in mind, in the back of his mind at all times, "Who am I?" So, I never agreed with "Who am I." The experiential awareness here is more, "What am I?" It seemed to me, "Who am I?" which was not notoriously successful, either, as a mantra, that "Who am I?" focuses you to look for another illusion, another definition, another pronoun as Self. That which is experienced as the identity with a personal transcended is a "what-ness." It's not a "who-ness." The "what-ness" has the peculiarity of sense of Self, with a capital *S*, but that Self is the "Allness of Everythingness," and it's really beyond "who-ness."

Some people who'd been there to his ashram, even after he died, you know, had said there was not a great deal of success with that method. And I always thought it's due to the "who-ness" rather than the "what-ness." We'll explain the "what-ness" to try and clarify what I just said.

So, as you're either in seated meditation or as you're walking about in the world, because as you progress in spiritual work, the two are not different; the two become the same. Because all of life, because of the way you recontextualize your life, becomes a meditation. So, on its highest level, then, a meditation is merely the manner in which you contextualize your experience of aliveness.

If you contextualize every instant of your existence as a dedication to the realization of God, your entire life becomes a meditation. So, we cannot separate out meditation as "this" and the "you" as "that," and a "this" and a "that." Meditation, then is a way of contextualizing your life, let's say, from a greater context, from a greater context.

You Are Not the Mind

What is witnessed, then, the body walking around on the stage, which is a peculiarity, actually, is merely the content of the field.

So, let's look at the field. Let's look at the field itself. So, the progressive fields of realization, whether you're walking about in a walking meditation throughout life, or whether you're seated, cross-legged, doing very specific breathing, picturing the energy flowing up your spine to the crown chakra and up to the higher levels, as light, uh-huh . . . or whether you're walking around in the world, the first thing that you experience is form. When a person sits down, they say, "Well, I can't seem to get any place with meditation, because the minute I sit down, the mind, the thoughts, are racing around"—the thoughts, the distractions of the world. And so, the average person's life, then, is focused on thought, form. The person bewails the fact that no matter what they do, their mind seems to be focused on the passing panorama of endless thoughts and feelings and form.

So, that is the first thing we notice. Now, because this form is endless, the content of thinkingness is endless. It goes on spontaneously. The first thing to notice about it is, it's got nothing to do with you, because you can tell it to stop and it won't. Well, if you were, if that's what you were and you told it to stop, it would instantly stop. So, you tell your mind, "Stop"; it goes right on thinking. It seems to be quite unruly. Those are the famous ox-herding pictures, you know. The first picture shows the ox, the wild ox. So, that's the wild, untamed mind, and the naïve person thinks, "Well, I have to deal with that." No, happily, you don't have to deal with the content of mind, because the only thing you have to notice about it is that what it's doing, it's doing spontaneously. It's not the content of mind that's interesting at all. What is of interest is the process of mind. It's going on *of its own*, has nothing to do with you. Couldn't care less about you. It will say very nasty things about you. You know what the mind does. "You're guilty, you're weak, you're wasting your money—you're a creep!" You can't trust the mind at all. It's not even your friend. It's not even a friend. I mean, it doesn't . . . it just goes on, and willy-nilly says all kinds of. . . . When it runs out of thoughts, it'll say, "Ippity bippity boo, roppity pop pop pop pop." It will take pictures of an erotic scene from some movie when you were a teenager. It'll think of something horrible about the future. Oh, my! When the mind gets threatened with no thoughts, it really gets wild; it'll just do anything crazy—think of stabbing yourself or something. You know, it'll just do anything bizarre to keep going.

So, when you look at the mind, then, don't be bothered with it. It's an endless phantasmagoria. I like that word—*phantasmagoria*. It just proliferates endless BS, you know, is what it's doing. Occasionally, occasionally, under very favorable circumstances, with great focus and effort, you can get it to stop all that and be—form a logical sequence for a short period of time and do what's called "thinking." Most of the time it's "thoughting," it's not thinking. It's "thoughting" and "imaging."

So, thinking, it does really quite rarely. "Should I turn left at the next corner?" It's through with thinking now; it's not going to think for another 20 minutes, probably. "Where shall I park?" That's the next time it thinks. What was it doing during that 20 minutes? It was, "Ippity bippity bob, bobla." "Three little fishies in a little bitty boo." That's the one my mind used to like, "three little fishies in an itty bitty boo."

All right. So, form then—the content is not of any interest. Now, many people spend endless spiritual lifetimes trying to change form. You realize how many spiritual programs have to do with form? "Don't think this; think that." "Recontextualize it this way." "Don't think of its opposite." You know, prefix it with "if," "but," "yes," or "no." Trying to change form is not going to work, because the ego, the mind is like the heartbeat, destined to do what it does. Why should the mind stop thinking when that's what it's supposed to do?

So, what does one realize out of this? If you watch the content of mind going by willy-nilly, like a madcap insane asylum, you realize that you are not the mind. If you were the mind and you told it to stop, it could stop. Hmm. We notice then, the first, most important thing that's going to take us out of it, is that it's impersonal. The most stunning thing to learn about witnessing the content of your mind is that it's impersonal. Like the heartbeat, like breathing, like your toenails growing—it's impersonal.

It doesn't ask you about it. Your toenails don't say, "Should I grow this month?" It's a sort of a physiologic spontaneous activity, thinkingness. So, don't be disturbed about it because it's doing what it's supposed to do. You can't really be worried about the content about it because no matter what trick you try with the content, it's smarter than you and it will trick you in some other way. You say, "Don't think about this." Good. It doesn't; it thinks about "that" instead.

So, the first thing you notice is that it's endless form and it's unstoppable. Trying to silence your mind is idiotic, and some people do that all the time. Trying to go to sleep at night and they're trying to stop their mind from thinking. What you notice is that it's impersonal; it does what it's doing of its own. Hmm. Wow! So, you stop identifying with the content of thought as "me." It's not "me." I can put you under hypnosis, program your mind; you wake up, you think all that, and you think, "I thought that." You didn't think that, idiot—I thought it.

So, the first thing we can notice, how do you know what the mind is thinking? How do you know? How do you know what— how do you know what's on that channel? You know it because it's registering. Ah! So, we're out of the content of mind, and now we'll say, "If I'm not the program, then maybe I'm the VCR." Well, you're getting closer. We're aware of what's going on in mind because it's registering somewhere. It's registering somewhere in consciousness, and it's being recognized. One of the functions of—you see, this mind is doing what it's doing, but that's not what's bothering you. What's bothering you is that you're registering it; you're aware of it. You're recognizing it, and who is doing that? The watcher is doing that. The experiencer is experiencing that the mind is doing all that. How do you know that the experiencer is experiencing? Because there's a watcher experiencing it, and below that, there is awareness.

So, the identifications of who I am, first as we sit in meditation or as we go about the day, is not the content of thought. It's not the content of feeling or thought or imaginations, or memories; it has to do closer with some impersonal function, called "registering."

Even recognition of—if you recognize a monkey as a monkey, that's not a decision that some personal "you" made. That happens of its own. So, that's trained, that's trained. So, these things are trained, they're impersonal; experiencing and watching is also impersonal. It's a phenomenon occurring of its own. So, you see, we begin withdrawing. It's like we draw back further and further from mentalization, more to the field. So, the field is watching, experiencing, and we become aware that this is impersonally happening within a field.

The Self, the Self is not the content. The Self, you become more aware of the Self as the awareness. And the awareness is coming out of an aspect of consciousness, the observer/witnesser. The observer/witnesser. You see, we're moving the sense of "I" from, "I am that bad person that forgot to fill the gas tank and ran out of gas. How could I be so stupid?" So, the naïve person identifies, then, with the content of thought itself. The average person is at the effect, is the victim of thinkingness. The average person is the victim of thought. They think, "That's who I am."

The next wondrous thing is, thought becomes imbued with preciousness. Thoughts are precious, wonderful, and we're enamored of them because they're "mine." We give thoughts great status because they're "*my* thoughts." If they were just "those" thoughts, they'd be easy to get rid of. But they're *my* thoughts. The minute we say, "*my*" thought, now it becomes precious and holy and we genuflect. They become precious. You hear people say they're worried that they might lose their memory. I mean, how lucky could you get? Wipe out a few years here and there, I mean, geez. You can always keep a couple of postcards, I mean, if you really want to remember it. I can't remember any years I wanna remember, frankly. I mean, the passing moment is bad enough without putting up with 75 years of all that.

I mean, it didn't start out too good right from the beginning. As I told you, here's this creepy, little kid body in a damn wagon—wow, I mean who wants to be bothered with that? Anyway, you're stuck with it. Not too happy from the first moment, to find out that you exist as a physicality.

So, you become more skeptical of mind. You start to distance yourself from mind. It becomes an "it" instead of a "me." It's a giant step when you realize the mind is an *it*; it's not a *me*. "To hell with you, mind! I reject you and disown you!" Denounce it as a fraud. It's a fraud! It comes on and it says, "I'm you." Boy, oh boy. Once you get suckered into that, the ego's really gotcha by the anh-anh, because now it's only a matter of what happens to go through your mind that you're the victim of. You go from strangulation, to suffocation, to guilt, to shame, to anxiety, regret— maybe you should kill yourself. It tells all kinds of people to kill themselves and they do. They do.

So, you don't wanna give it power over yourself. Wow! You give it power by giving it reality. And you give it power by calling it "me." By giving it identification as the reality of the self, the precious, wonderful me; my wonderful feelings. They become sacred. The mind becomes God. You worship the ego/mind. Modern society worships the mind. It's given up on God, and religion, and instead it worships science. The salvation of man was once thought to be the province of God and religion. Salvation of man has now been allocated to science and computers: science, computers, and bureaucracies. The government announces a new bureaucracy every few months. It's going to solve everything. Except the next one is going to be just as incompetent as the last one. Why? Because the structure, the structure is such that it guarantees failure. Bureaucracy is one layer of structure on top of another, until finally you become completely immobilized. People think the end of the world is going to be a big bang. No, the end of the world is going to come when everything comes to a stop because the complexity has become so overwhelming that everything just succumbs to the sheer complexity. Eventually, the tax form gets so long that even if you start on January first, you can't finish it by December 31, and the tax people aren't going to stop.

The FBI, we knew what was wrong with the FBI before it happened, but I said to Susan, I said, "Under this much complexity of bureaucratic relations, you know, even if a bomb was allowed to go off in the bathroom, they wouldn't be able to do anything about it. You've got to get permission from this department, and you've got to fill out this form to get permission, you've got to get through the layers. By that time, the bathroom's blown up, see."

So, the mind then becomes a tyrant, the tyrant. And it creates a delusion. The delusion is that "I am my thoughts; I am the mind; I'm it. That's where my power is, that's where my destiny is. My memory of mind is more precious than anything else." And then you fear what's going to happen in mind in the future. So, mind is really the most difficult thing of spiritual awareness.

We start out with the form. We become aware that we are not the mind, so the first thing you do with meditation or in reflection—I'm going to talk today—we're talking about meditation, but to a considerable extent, it's reflection and contemplation, because if you do meditation continuously, you can now label it as something else. You can call it contemplation and reflection, which is quite heavily Christian. Christianity doesn't go too much for sitting down and shaving your head and going "Om" and focusing on the tip of your nose. Christianity is more contemplating the truth of the great spiritual teachers as you go about your business and instituting them in your daily affairs. Be kind and considerate and thoughtful and gentle and patient. So, the Christian virtues become more the field of contemplation in which one lives one's life, and by which one judges one's actions. And it's not really a formal meditation as such. We're going to blend the two so that contemplation becomes the formal meditation that allows you to meditate throughout the day, no matter what you're doing, just as I'm doing at this moment.

So, the first realization is that one is not one's thoughts. One's thoughts are like a curse. I shouldn't say that. That sounds too severe. One's thoughts are like bad luck. Bad luck! You see, the core of the ego's narcissism. You get this, the narcissistic core of the ego is the sense of "I," coming out of the source of the ego itself. It's a sense, it's, um, it's a sense of authority, it's a sense of . . . I can't get the right word. It'll come. Your thinkingness, the naïve person thinks that the thinkingness is who they are. They become, then, at the effect of this thinkingness. They are subject to it. They are the victim of this thinkingness. They begin to hate the content of their own thinkingness, and they begin to hate themselves, because they think that thinkingness is who they are. "I have bad thoughts."

I told you once before I was brought up High Episcopal. On Saturday afternoon you had to go to confession, so you waited as long as possible on Friday afternoon. Last confession was four o'clock, so there would be as little time as possible between confession and communion in the morning. If you go to confession late and go to early communion, the chances of sinning in the meantime are statistically much reduced. You lived in fear that this spot on your soul would appear, you know. "O, Lord, I'm sorry for this, that, the other, and you do the rosary, you do the whole thing, the Our Fathers, the Hail Marys. You keep your eyes focused on the ground. Careful control of your thoughts and your mind that you won't have a sinful thought, get to seven o'clock communion, you can make it probably from five on Saturday to seven o'clock on Sunday morning without a sin. A spot on your soul, which God could see. And just as you're on your way to church with the top down on the '29 Model A Ford, you pass a 42 ft. x 96 ft. advertisement of Jantzen swimsuits. Here's this big, blonde lady, 42 feet long—there goes the innocence. At age six it wouldn't bother you, but at 14, it was. . . 32-foot-long swimming suit. I won't ever forget. Nowadays, you would consider her fully dressed, but in those days. . . .

So, we live in fear then of the content of mind because it's labeled with guilt. Sin and guilt are primarily labeled mentally, all right. So, the first thing to realize is "I am not the content of mind." You see, you look at yourself, you realize you live in terror of your own mind. What's our percentage on that? Everybody live in terror of their mind? Yeah, everybody lives in terror of their mind. Everybody lives in fear and terror of the mind. What craziness is it going to think up next? What fear? What guilt? Dear Lord, protect us from the mind. Forget about enemies. Enemies are a nice diversion. They take you out of your mind. If somebody's there threatening to kill you, man that's cool, because you're out of the whole sweat and worry thing.

You've just gotta deal with this guy, you know what I'm saying? That's true. When I've been in life-threatening situations, I mean, you know, you're out of it. So, we stop registering, then, with the content of consciousness. We begin to realize that form, that processing form, is what it does. It's like a little computer and you can't shut it off. It's just going all the time with the images, you know; it goes on all the time.

It's not "I." "I" would have to be something beyond it in order to witness it. "I" would have to at least be on the level of witness. Who knows what goes on in the mind and complains about the mind, unless they were witnessing it? And they couldn't witness it, so what they complain about is what they're observing. But the pain comes from identifying with it. So, the first thing you do with meditation, either as contemplation as you go about the day, or sitting formal meditation, is to realize that to withdraw from the content of mind and realize that "That which I am" is what is witnessing it. The witnesser, the witness, the observer is happening of its own. The light of consciousness, then, is what one begins to identify with. One is that which witnesses the mind. First you say, I'm that which experiences—first you say, "I am the mind." Then you say, no, I can't be the mind; I must be the experiencer of the mind. I must be the witness of the mind. But what is witnessing and watching doing?

It's Happening of Its Own

Well, witnessing and watching are also happening of their own. I want you to see these things are impersonal. See, when you identify with mind, you say, "I am that"—that's personal. It's not personal—it's happening of its own. You can't stop it from doing that. Breathing is not personal. Decide you're going to quit and see how long it works!

You begin to identify, then, with the field instead of the content. You're the space in which all this is happening. It is consciousness itself which is lighting up the awareness of all that's happening. You realize that which does not change from moment to moment, that which does not change from moment to moment must be what your reality is. Your reality can't be that which changes every second because you would like a flickering image on the screen, constantly changing. That which does not change, which is always present. When you first wake up in the morning, all you're aware of is that you are. If you watch the waking phenomena, out of oblivion comes awareness of "is-ness." The minute you start becoming conscious, if I stop you and say, "What do you know?" "Ah, I'm awake." "What does awake mean?" "I'm conscious that I'm conscious." You're conscious that you're conscious. That's all you're conscious of. "What is your name?" "Uhh." "What's the date?" "Uhh, uhh." "Where are you going today?" "I don't know." That all comes later after you have coffee. The first awareness is that you are, so the ultimate and infinite context then is existence itself, to be aware of existence. That which I am is that out of which existence arises, not the content of existence, not the content. Otherwise, you'd be different because you had a haircut today, you know, you can't be the content.

The sense of Self, the identification of "who am I," with meditation and contemplation, we'll talk more about it, as how the techniques work. Progressively, you no longer say, "this is I," you no longer say, "this is I," you no longer say, "this is I." The sense of "I" withdraws, to become progressively the field itself. Progressively, one realizes that that which "I" am is the capacity for consciousness. I'm not even consciousness. The infinite capacity to be conscious, I am prior to consciousness itself. That which I am is before consciousness. Consciousness is willy-willy crap stuff. Late in the game. Small fry, like a mouse. That which you are is beyond consciousness. It's because of what you are consciousness can spring forth as an awareness, as a volitional awareness. The sense of Self—realize that you are beyond consciousness itself. If it weren't for what you are, consciousness couldn't field itself. Couldn't field itself into what? It has to have existence. So, don't sell yourself short. You're the infinite potentiality out of which consciousness arises, out of which all the rest of this BS passes itself off as you, due to the illusion of the ego, because the ego is narcissistic and it's in love with itself. When you see the ego for what it is, it thinks you're wonderful. Your thoughts are wonderful. Even if they aren't wonderful thoughts, they're important thoughts—Christ! Because your catastrophes are mind-boggling. This exaggeratedness is the magnification that the ego creates out of narcissism. So, what holds the whole ego together, then, is that one enamored of oneself, enamored.

The ego then takes credit for being who you are. It also takes credit that it's the author of your existence. It succeeds most of the time. Most of the time. Eighty-five percent of the population it succeeds *big* time. Big time. What I think and what I feel is more important than all of humanity. Can you believe the ego can be that big? Narcissism, grandiosity, megalomania can reach such a great dimension? To the average person, it's not even imaginable. That you could get up front in a world court and say that what you want for your country is more important than the lives of all the countrymen. What?! This is not a crime; this is a mental illness. A mental illness. So, the egotism of the ego is unlimited. Unlimited.

To think, you know—God isn't God, I'm God. The refusal to surrender the authority for the source of one's own existence to God is what gets you there.

So, meditation quickly, before long, brings about a certain degree of humility. You realize that I'm not the content of thought. In fact, I can't even manage it for more than a couple of seconds. The source of the sense of self then progressively withdraws from specificity and form, becomes progressively more diffuse, more general, becomes the light of consciousness itself, eventually becomes the allness out of which the unmanifest manifests itself as manifestation. The infinite reality. The infinite reality is the infinite potentiality. The power of God is infinite because God is infinite context. Out of infinite context arises all power and the potentiality for existence in form or non-form. And that's our reality; that's what we are. Potentiality to become conscious, because you can choose.

As you walk about in the world, then, there's less and less focus on content. I warn you in advance, it gets you into trouble. It gets you into trouble sometimes. You don't know where the hell the light switch is. How do you work this fan? I don't know. Because in youth, you're focused on thingness, you know. All the gadgets, the electronic gadgets that crowd the marketplace now are made by insane 24-year-olds, who are crazy about the electronics, and you just can't buy a clock, an alarm clock, you know what I'm saying? You can't just go "on/off." You can't buy a radio that just goes "on/off." I've got a radio in my waiting room that's worth its price in gold. It's got a dial like that, and then it's got "on, "off," "volume." I turn it, it goes on; I tune it to WRFM—there you go. All set. Somebody gave me one for Christmas, oh my God. It's got an instruction manual this thick. It's fine print. Anything made in Japan or China has to have very fine print. "Push button A six times, then push button B, wait three seconds and push button and then go 8-6-9-4-2." By doing that you can set your alarm clock to go on and off on Tuesday, Thursday, Friday, and Saturday and alternate weeks on the following weeks. And I don't know how to use it. I put it back in the box, and I've got boxes full of wonderful presents, made up by 22-year-olds. Wonderful watches, but I can't figure out how to use them. I don't know how to use them. So, what you do is catch the nearest 22-year-old and say, "How do you turn this thing on?" To them, it's simple. All right. So, that to me is the world of form. The world of form is mind-boggling, complex, tiring. I mean, I'm tired just to look at the instruction manual. And you're supposed to send in a registration card. I never do that—it's horrible. A warranty card. If it breaks down, forget it, you know. I'm not going to send it back to the company and get my 17 dollars back. I mean you know what I'm saying? Blow a whole afternoon doing that? Go back and forth to the post office, package this thing up, "I want my seventeen dollars," write them a letter, fill out the form, have it signed, affidavit, witnessed. You know what I'm saying? I'm just giving you my warped view of what the world calls "reality." I want you to keep in mind that my view is warped. Abnormal, according to the world. Because the world loves form and loves the detail of form, you know.

I get more of the context. I want the gist of a thing. I can walk into a room—instantly, I've got what it's all about, what everybody's there about, what the whole scene is about, what the sense of it is about, what the prevailing energy field is; therefore, what to expect, what's possible; you know, the upside, the downside; potentiality; what's already happened; what's likely to happen; you can almost see the future of it arising and you can see how it all arose. You can see how it all came together throughout time and where it is this passing moment, and you can see where it's going. That's what you want is the essence. You can read the essence in one split second. We all learn to do that. Certain neighborhoods in New York City, if you don't know how to do that, you ain't going to live long. You can just tell by the ambiance as you turn the corner! Hmm, I think I'll go this way. You don't know why. We call it intuition, don't we?

So, that which is not in form within you, as you become progressively aware of it, you become more and more what we call "intuitive." You just "read" it. I've told you before, I remember walking down Tenth Avenue in New York City late at night, and I could tell by the footsteps behind me, half a block behind me. I knew from the footsteps what it was, what it had in mind, what it intended, what my fate would be if I didn't read it right, and I crossed over the street. All right. So, the animal learns that, so that capacity, that innate capacity to focus on context instead of content is learned. You've already got the capacity. The animal knows it. The animal as it turns the corner also knows uh-oh! It senses the lion up in the tree and walks the other way, to live another day. If it fails to, it's gone. Bye-bye. Water buffalo. So.

We have the capacity, then, to focus either centrally when we need to, or peripherally. With spiritual evolution, one becomes progressively the field. One is the field. Understand? All of us, we are the field here. We're the field out of which the field then brings forth the talkingness of the content through this speaker. You know what I'm saying? That's happening spontaneously of its own. It has nothing to do with any personal self. I'd have to stop and think what am I going to say. That would be like looking through the construction book on an electronic gadget, you know what I'm saying? You can get a general thrust of what we'll talk about today, but then it happens of its own. Because it's happening as a result of the field. And the field is set by the consciousness level of the people here and their intention and their interest. That's what creates a sense of the field.

So, one becomes aware "I'm the field," the infinite potentiality, the Buddha nature, the Buddha nature. The Buddha nature is the unmanifest, potentiality. It is beyond form, but it is not void, because it is the infinite potentiality. Out of the infinite potentiality is Allness, not nothingness. If you go the way of negation, you'll end up like I did lifetime after lifetime in the stupid void, and you come back here, wham! You've got a freaky body in a wagon to put up with. The physicality, the shock.

No, the ultimate reality is not void nothingness. If it was nothingness, I wouldn't be back. I've been in the void. What is it that witnesses the void? Who's to talk about void? If void is the ultimate reality, no one would know of it, would they? It would be like brain wipeout. Who's going to tell you that their brain got wiped out? Nobody. Nothing there. Because the Ultimate Reality is the Unmanifest, it becomes manifest as the infinite potentiality of consciousness itself, which is then capable of all this content— all this content and thinkingness. Let's see if what we said is true: "That depiction is aligned with God's truth—resist." [True.] "We have permission to ask in front of this audience—resist." [True.] "It's over 999." [True.] "It's 1,000." [True.] "1001." [Not true], 1,000. It's the absolute understanding of which we are capable in this dimension, that which was just said is the absolute, infinite, ultimate capacity of comprehension of one's reality. It comes out of the realization of the truth that one is the infinite, infinite potentiality. So, you start thinking of yourself as the infinite potentiality to have the experiencer who's temporarily identifying with the bodyness at someplace called Sedona or something. But that's all just possible because of the infinite potentiality.

So, here we have, then, what we arrived at just by playing with it in your mind. You just play with it in your mind as you get up in the morning; you start with being just the infinite space for this day to happen in; that's what you really are, see? You start out as the unmanifest, which then becomes manifest and says, "Yes, oh, it's me." I say, "Who are you when you wake up?" "I don't know . . . uh, I mean, I'm George." "And what are you doing today, George?" "Well, uh . . . uh." It takes you a while to get who you are. So, this state here is not different than a state which you are already familiar with, huh?

The capacity to relate to the field instead of the content of the field. I don't know if it's good to do that when you're driving, when you're first starting this. Maybe it is—I don't know. But having been a cab driver, you know you're in that space, and you just automatically, you know, you just automatically beat the other guy to the fare standing at the curb without thinking about it. How can one function in that state? Well, there may be truthfully so, there's some impairments. I really don't know how to work those crazy clocks, and you know what? I don't care about them, because I'm not that interested in what time it is, anyway, to begin with. But the world is, so you better know what time it is. But you need some kind of a clock, you know. You need an old-fashioned clock. You can even wind the thing, you know. There is perhaps some loss of detail of life. However, the potentiality to appreciate the detail is constantly there. It's constantly there.

So, that's one way. That's the way starting from peripheral vision. The "everywhereness," the Allness, "beyond-timeness." You see that it has nothing to do with now. All kinds of books about "now." Lord, save us from "now." Thank you, Sir. If there's no "then" and no "when" and no future and no past, and there is not any "now" either. There's no point to try to focus on the moment of "now" in meditation. People say, "I try to focus on 'now,' but I can't focus on 'now'; my mind's always thinking about the past or the future." Your mind's always thinking about the past or the future, right now, isn't it? So, you're still in the "now" even if you're thinking about the past or the future. But "now" is just a label we put to a specific awareness. Let's say, because your awareness happens to be passing this point, it says, "this is now," "this is now," "this is now," "this is now." That's just a nominalization. Your mind just made that up. There isn't any "now-ness" going on, folks. Let's not walk around saying we live in the "now." That's a corruption of reality. Nobody lives in any "now." Show me the "now" you live in, idiot. You don't live in any "then," you don't live any "future," you don't live in any "now" either. All those are time dimensions. Those are all durations. Those are all depictions. Those are all nominalizations which arise up in here, see; you've got to give it a name. Why do you have to give a name to whatever is at this second? You see? And when you get to a certain level, you don't even call it "is" anymore. That's also an absurdity. There's neither "is" nor "is not."

The conundrum at age three was "existence" versus "nonexistence." There's this horrid little body in this rotten little wagon, and instantly comes the fear. First of all, the kid couldn't think in words; this was all nonverbal. But awareness is aware of this existence. Along with existence came instantly fear of nonexistence. It was apparent that if one "is," it could have come about that one "is not"—would not have been. You know what I'm saying? If you could "be," it could have happened that your coming into being-ness wouldn't have happened, in which case, you "wouldn't be." At age three I'm puzzling "existence" versus "nonexistence." A fear of nonexistence. Oh, boy, oh, boy.

So, the first thing existence does is give you fear of nonexistence. We see that in the ego's concern with death. It thinks that it dies; it's not going to exist anymore. Folks, no such thing's going to happen. No such luck. You don't go from existence to nonexistence. You just go to a different style of existence, in which all these lifetimes string out as one lifetime. I went through a couple of them the other day. Oh, my God, I'd just as soon forget that altogether, but it was how consciousness evolved through these various physicalities, each one serving a very definite purpose. And, as I say, they tended to flip-flop. In this one, you did this and the next lifetime you flip back again to like, undo all that. Oh, boy. All right.

So, the way out of all of that, the karmic constant—see, because when you're in that lifetime, you forgot that. And you remember it again and wham! Because as long as one is identifying with form, then you're going to keep reincarnating; there's no way beyond it; I can see that. As long as you think, "I am anything specific," that specificness will then create a new specificness. Once you realize you're the field of the infinite potentiality, you're beyond it. You think you want another lifetime? I've got news for you. When you get there, you're not going to like any better than you like this lifetime. I look back at previous lifetimes, I didn't like any one of them any better than any other one. On a certain level they were all horrid. On a certain level, they were all exciting. On a certain level they were all everything else, and I can do without it. After you've had enough lifetimes, I mean, you can do without them. You just don't have a yen for another lifetime, folks. Like you've gone and seen so many movies.

I'm not interested in movies. I never watch movies. I mean, I've seen them all. I've seen every twist and turn and writer's fantasy about how he can phrase this to express that. I've seen every actor's and actress's doing it there. And I just don't get it entertaining anymore.

Enlightenment, then, would be dissolution of the identification with content. With content. With existence as form. Even with existence itself. That which I am is beyond existence. Existence came out of that which I am. Just as consciousness arose out of that which . . . you can't be at the effect of anything. There's nothing causing anything. Consequently, anything phrased within the context of causality cannot be the absolute reality. Inasmuch as one lifetime does not karmically cause the next lifetime, no. Something outside of all of those lifetimes tends to bring them into physical manifestation. You can't be the content of each lifetime; you have to be the source out of which those lifetimes are arising, and one is re-choosing reincarnation.

Contemplation, then, is just walking about, and you see you can do it right now. Just be aware. Forget about what the speaker's talking about. He just chatters on and talks and talks. And the room if full of what appears to be people and all that. And you realize that the capacity to be aware of the phenomena, so if we look at it phenomena-logically, the capacity to be aware of the phenomena is what you are. You hold the capacity. What you are is the capacity to be aware of any of this. You can pay as much attention to it as you want. See, that's volitional. You can either pay attention to it, you can identify with it, or not identify with it.

Even to say what day it is, is a mentation. It's no day right now, at all. There is no day that it is today, anymore than there is any month that it is today, or year that it is today. Those are all made-ups, just wordingnesses, conveniences. In the world of form, that's very convenient to say, "I'll see you Wednesday." Okay. If you live in non-form, there isn't any Wednesday. The world says, "Wednes-day," you see. Okay, you say it's Wednesday, I'll go on Wednesday. You can go along with the world, but it's elective. That's the difference—it's elective. If you're not at the effect of it. Otherwise, you're suffering from Mondayness, Tuesdayness, Wednesdayness.

* * *

It's very easy to get that you are beyond that which is any physical-ity. The infinite awareness is radiating forth as a seeming phenom-enon. But you get that you're beyond all that. You get that you're the field out of which consciousness arises. Is that so? Everybody agree? We're all the infinite field out of which consciousness arises. We're not the product of consciousness; we're its capacity, its source, out of which consciousness arises. The manifest arises out of the unmanifest. Creation arises out of the unmanifest and be-comes manifest in what the world calls evolution, which is the ap-pearance that creation takes. By sequential observation, it seems like there's sequence. The sequence is not in the out-thereness, the sequence is in the perception. Sequential perception creates the il-lusion of causality. There isn't any cause out there at all, folks.

When I was a kid, I lived out in the country, and the only way to get to school was to hitchhike—10 below 0—it was a lonely highway, and anyway, the only hope for a ride was an occasional car and occasional truck. So, you hear the truck coming about a mile away, you know, and get all excited. As the truck got closer and closer, I had a little magical thing I would do to make the truck stop and pick me up. I'd go, "Seven, seven, seven, seven, seven,

seven, seven." I'd do it seven times and turn around seven times. And that would make the truck stop. So, I'd do that, and then the truck would spot me, and I could hear him hitting the airbrake, kchew, kchew. Half a mile away he'd start and hit the airbrakes because on the icy snow, he'd better start hitting them early. So, here's this kid out there with his books, you know, and in those days, you know, everybody sort of trusted everybody. Nowadays you'd think he was probably a killer or something, but anyway, in those days everybody trusted everybody. So, the truck driver would pick up this kid standing out in the cold wind and snow, you know. But the idea of magic was of course that saying seven, seven, seven times and spinning about my heels seven times was going to make this truck stop, you know. Of course, when it did, that connected the magic even stronger. And once in a while, it wouldn't. Well, still, it happened a lot of the time, but you see how your mind gives causality to it.

So, we want to get out of that child's world, then, of magical causality. The world's belief in causality is really sort of magic— living the world of magic, because it doesn't see that what it takes to create every instant is the totality of God as Creation through- out all of time. So, we get out of being the content of conscious- ness. We become the context of consciousness. We become the reality out of which consciousness arises.

A Few Specifics about Meditation

I want to just go into a few more specifics about meditation and handling content of mind. And things to notice about it. If you sit in formal meditation and focus on the content of mind as it passes by, the first thing you notice is it's irrational; it goes on and on, and then you begin to see that the thinkingness is coming about as a result of several things: habit, boredom, the idea that thoughts are worthwhile; that they serve a purpose, so they're entertain- ment; they're going to solve problems; thinkingness is something you can do. People think thinking is worthwhile—"I'm going to sit down and think about that." But when you're meditating, you're not interested—what you're interested in is getting beyond thought.

There is a field of energy out of which thinkingness is arising. And so, I want to go into a specific detail about that. Let's say you're sitting in formal meditation and the thinkingness is arising of its own. You'll see it's arising of its own. It's coming out of a desire to think. The mind wants to think. It's coming out of an energy. If you don't get caught up in the content of thought, you end up at a point of observation where the thinkingness arises, and then it passes away. I think we said at a previous lecture, like looking out a car window without focusing on what's going by but looking through the same point of the car window, everything flicks by, you understand what I'm saying? You know, like fixate on this and watch it, and then fixate on the next. That's the way the mind usually works. And the eyes. It looks at this and then it follows it, and then it clicks back this way and clicks, constantly doing that.

There is a way of focusing on thought of not moving with the thought, not getting absorbed in the content, the emotion, the story of it. Just witnessing from a fixed point of observation that the thought arises. A specific thought arises out of sort of amorphous potentiality to become a thought. It gains greater and greater form. It becomes very, very specific, crosses the point of attention, it begins to fade out. It loses form and disappears. There's a form of meditation which requires one-pointedness of thought. This is out of Zen training. There is a fixity of intention of one-pointedness of mind to focus so, like a razor, on the edge of this moment of focus. So, the thought arises like a note of music arises, crests; no sooner does the note of music crest than the music is already fading away. You become aware with this fixity of intention and focus, that that which is the self is prior to the thought. That that which one is arises from the source. You see all the thinkingness is coming out of an energy, and one can then begin to release the energy of the desire to think. Let's see how that works. I haven't done it in some years.

This thought is arising out of a formless energy field which begins to gather form, becomes specific as a thought, and then fades away. One can, by fixity of focus, fix on the instant, let's say, we'll use the term *instant* on the process, just prior to its coming into form. In the beginning, you start thinking about your old dog Rover, and how he got glaucoma in his left carbuncle and you had to take him to the vet, and under anesthesia he croaked, and the family cried and good old Rover, and Christ, now what are we going to do for a dog? I mean, you got this whole long story. As you meditate, you get beyond that, and you get to see Rover . . . okay, I mean, you picture Rover's image. There's perhaps a slight memory, but now you get to Roverness itself. I mean, there's the essence of Roverness without the whole freaky story that goes with Roverness. There's just the essence of Roverness. And now, the name Rover disappears. You just focus on the essence of that dog's beingness and its lovingness. You get to the heart of what was Rover, and now the form is disappearing. You're getting almost to dog-ness. You're getting to animal-relatedness. You're getting to life identifying with life. You're getting to an energy that is prior to the specific of thought itself. Those specific thoughts are coming out of like a little energy factory, a little energy source, energy sync, whatever you call it. And one can surrender that to God.

We didn't talk about renunciation yet. Surrender, then, is renunciation, in that one eventually lets go of the belief that one is the source of all that and sees that it is happening of its own. One lets go of the wantingness of thinkingness. Early in the game you see that thinkingness all has a payoff. The way to silence that thinkingness is to be willing to surrender the payoff of that thinkingness. The sad stories, the excitement, the erotic titillation, whatever is associated with that thought. The willingness to surrender that. The great pleasure of being right. Judgmentalism. Righteousness. The downfall of mankind since the beginning of time has been righteousness. Everybody feels righteous in what they do. Everybody that pulls the trigger on you feels righteous. Every war is based on righteous. Everybody's righteous . . . I don't want to hear about people's rights and righteousness. Give me a break.

So, the mind wants to be righteous; it wants to manufacture self-pity, grief, mourning, anger, rage, delight, anticipation, fear. It does a whole melodrama. One has to be willing to let go the payoff of these ego positionalities. First, you discern, what is the payoff of that? Well, it's the fun of hating those idiots. We love to hate people. I mean, it's fun, isn't it? They're bad and they deserve it, so. . . .

To start to silence the mind, we witness how it behaves, then we see that it's being sourced, it's being sourced by the payoff of this thinkingess. As we're willing to surrender the payoff to God, could you let go the pleasure of self-pity and surrender it to God? Could you? Yeah. Would you? Okay. So, there's a constant of let-goingness of the payoff of this thinkingness. That gives the thinkingness less of an emotional charge. The willingness to surrender the payoff. Each negative feeling is not serving something else; it's serving itself. The payoff of guilt is that you get to feel guilty. The payoff of anger is you get angriness. You get to experience the payoff. The feeling *is* the payoff. People say, "What do people get out of hate?" Well, you get hatred, man, what do you think? That's why we killed all those kids at school. Bang, bang, bang! The gratification is the feeling itself. You see, our society can't find the answer to anything because it's always trying to psychologize everything and look for the reason in childhood. There isn't any reason in childhood. It's the glee of it now.

Watch the TV, then, in the Middle East throwing rocks at each other. This side throws rocks at this side; they're really getting off on that. This side then throws rocks on that side. They got off on that too. Now, they both get indignant. Boy, they're all hot with indignity. And they pull out rifles and shoot away at each other and throw bombs, and then they send in tanks and blast away. And then someone gets on TV about the poor little infant, the poor mother crying. It's all melodrama, such a huge payoff. I mean, how can you resist it? So, the mind gets sucked into it and it can't get out. You don't have to look for something from childhood to explain it. The payoff is in the instant of now. It's right now is the payoff. The payoff of rage is you get to feel rage. Watch those people throwing rocks at each other. It's a state of high glee. Isn't it? It's got nothing to do with their childhood. It's got nothing to do with politics; it's got nothing to do with America being richer and all that crap. They just love an excuse to throw rocks. So, the payoff is the experience itself.

In meditation we have to be willing to surrender the payoff of the experience itself to God. "Lord God, out of my worship of Thee, my desire and love to be of service, I am willing to relinquish the payoff of this emotionality, so that I can get beyond it." That's it.

So, that way the thinkingness has less of an emotional charge, because as long as you're getting off on the charge of the emotion of the thinkingness, it's not going to stop. If you can reduce the emotion behind it now, it slows down and it becomes more available for inspection. So, a great deal of what's done in formal meditation, at least in Zen style one-pointedness of mind, is inspection. One inspects the phenomena of thinkingness. We know that the minute you inspect a thing, it already changes. Nisargadatta Maharaj said that. That when you start observing the mind, it already begins to change out of observation. Observation. So, the first thing that's happening in meditation is by the mere act of observation you are already altering the content of consciousness by virtue of your intention. To get to the source of this thinkingness if you follow this tract of one-pointed fixity of observation, you'll get that all thinkingness is coming out of a little energy factory like a little source of a volcano, and one can surrender the anlage of the thought before it takes form. As you keep letting it go, it starts out with a story about good old Rover. As you let go that whole story, it gets down to just a paragraph. As you let go the paragraph, it gets down to a sentence. Finally, it just gets down to the name Rover. The willingness to surrender the instant a thing arises in consciousness, you find even "Rover" starts to dissolve. You start to think Ro—just before it becomes Rover.

First the long story, sad story, you're weeping and crying all about Rover, now this story is just down to barely remembering the name Rover. Now it just comes up as Ro-, then R, the image of a dog arises, doesn't have a name yet, not even Rover. You don't allow it to get to the point of Roverness. You'll see that being willing to surrender the intentionality of thinkingness itself can be surrendered at its very root. At its very root. At that point, the mind becomes silent, and one is that out of which thinkingness arises. This is possible scientifically. Talk about erudition, man, like you hit it today.

How do we focus this guy on this thing? It takes energy to focus on the world, I tell you. I mean, focusing on form is de-energizing. I don't know how people do it or how they get away with it. Focusing on form is exhausting, you know what I mean? You've got to pay attention to what they're saying, aw gee. I'd rather get it, "Can you say that in three words or less?" Anybody who wants a conversation with me, if you can make it in a couple of sentences, I'll be glad to talk to you. If you want to tell me all about your aunt Matilda, and all what went on in your three pregnancies and the husbands that came and went, I really can't handle it.

Let's get to the *essence*. Truth is very, very brief, you know. The absolute truth is absolutely wordless. So, those of you who wish to speak to me in a wordless style, God bless you! You just come up to me and you give me the thought like that—I got it! Okay, so, no, you're okay, I just got to. . . . All right, so you get beyond thinkingness.

How can this be? How can you get beyond thinkingness? I mean, are we talking mysterious fiction, or what?

We haven't talked much about quantum mechanics, but the book *Power vs. Force* has to do with going from the linear to the nonlinear paradigm, linear to nonlinear. In the book I'm finishing now, it has, in the back, a precis of quantum mechanics, for anybody that's interested in it. It's an incredible and wonderful and exciting subject. Anyway, what's interesting about quantum mechanics is that, as you're all aware, as you get to smaller and smaller submicroscopic, sub-particles, subatomic, sub-electrons, sub-photonic reality, that consciousness has an *observable* effect. You're all aware of the Heisenberg principle, correct? Everybody?

Anybody doesn't know what it is? All right, so we'll give the basic experiment that gives the whole thing away.

When an atom of matter and one of anti-matter meet, they extinguish each other, and when they do, there's a discharge of two photons. The photons head off in different directions in the universe. They have no spin to them. However, if a human being looks at one photon, *shew*—it instantly begins to spin. At the same time, on the opposite side of the universe, with no connection between the two whatsoever, the other photon begins to spin in exactly the opposite direction at exactly the same instant. The mere act of observation, witnessing, changes reality. So, that's the space in which prayers are effective, meditation, the space in which that which you hold in mind tends to manifest, energy follows thought, all the spiritual realities that we know, that prayer is effective, that meditation. . . . Ah, how can I see when I'm standing in my own light? This thing is not working too good here. The world—I don't know—it's such a crazy place.

All right, so we can compare. This is the world of logic, the linear reality of quantum reality. Last night there was a program on near-death experiences, you know. It starts out very good and then deteriorates to where he tries to negate that it has any spiritual reality, because his consciousness is stuck over here in the Newtonian paradigm, and although these people profess to be scientists, I say to them, "Have you heard of quantum mechanics?" Because they're still coming from, you know, 50 years ago—if it's not measurable. . . .

So, this is the ordinary reality of ordinary life. The Newtonian paradigm, in which things are logical, sequential—where's the word *cause*? Good gosh, I forgot the word *cause*, man. This is an orderly, everything is caused, logically, predictably, look back to your childhood to find out why you do things is reductionist. It's provable; it's measurable; everything is sequential, temporal; you can figure it out on a computer; it's solvable by the differential calculus. It's based on force. Everything is finished. It's a subtle world that you can count on. It'll also kill you. Anyway, the discovery of advanced theoretical physics, then, has to do with quantum reality, the quantum. And the mathematics of it is somewhat complicated. You don't have to go into the Schrödinger equations to understand the infinite quantum potentiality. But, as we get smaller and smaller, this has to do with the macroscopic world. This is the world of grossness, but you and I are aware that the subtle feelings of "is-ness," existence, the subtleties, and inferences, are not on the level of the gross; they're not on the level of the measurable. They don't even, you know, don't even exist in time or space because the Ultimate Reality is *subjective*. The Ultimate Reality is subjective.

This is where power resides [the Quantum side]. Power is in the context, not in the content. This is the finished product [Newtonian side]; this is the end of it all. This is the consequence. It ends up as the Empire State Building. This is the Empire State Building. Where did the Empire State Building come from? A guy was sitting there, probably smoking a Camel cigarette back in the '30s. The tallest building in the world, you know. The tallest building in New York City. The tallest building in the world. And the thing begins to grow in his mind, and it grows, and it grows, and the more he thinks about it, the more excited he gets. Then a design begins to form in his head. It's all starting over here [Quantum side]. It was poised; it was a potentiality; it's all uncertain, purely subjective. It's expansive; it grows with possibilities; it's unlimited—he could have made it twice as tall, right? When this is going to arise, either in thought or in the world is stochastic, it's not predictable. If we knew all these factors, and in the back of the book, the current book, I put an index in which you can look at all these factors; they all have mathematical names, of whether it's time-dependent or independent. These are two different Schrödinger equations, to solve these two different equations. As you can see, you're dealing with potentiality. You're dealing with things that are observable, but not measurable. They're comprehensible. They're not local any place. Where's the locality of the Empire State Building before it goes into physicality? It's nowhere; it's diffuse. It's intermingled with thoughts of New York City and the glamour of the city and the glory of man, and it's a progressive, imaginative, creative, free, unpredictable, illogical, disorderly, infinite potentiality. There is the infinite potentiality of context, out of which what we call 'Reality' arises. It's the infinite potentiality of consciousness itself. It's idiotic, then, for anybody to take a position that this [Quantum side] is unreal and this [Newtonian side] is real. Because it's only out of the subjectivity of what they call the unreal, that you can say that the objective world exists. No statement about objectivity has any validity except as a subjective reality. So, the Absolute, Infinite Reality is subjectivity.

The presence of God within expresses itself as the infinite potentiality out of which arises subjective awareness as consciousness. The presence is radically *sub-jec-tive.* It's not "out there," elsewhere, some other time, for other people. The average religious concept of God is—God arose somewhere back there in time, spun the dice, now he's disappeared, up there with his feet up, in an easy chair, waitin' for time to end, at which time we're going to have Judgment Day—oh, whoa! So, God's waiting elsewhere, in time and space; heaven is up there someplace. Astronauts have been up there; they haven't found any heaven up there. Where is heaven? God is elsewhere in time and place. How can you experience a God which isn't even here? *"Was"* and *"will be,"* but is not *"now,"* huh? The God of Judgment Day. So, God disappears, creates the dice, takes off, and now the world, how does it keep going?

It goes like billiard balls, supposedly causality, so the explanation, then, of what the world considers Reality is over here [Newtonian side]. Actually, the explanation is over here [Quantum side]. Here is where the explanation is. So, any concept of objectivity, then, is a *subjective* judgment. There is no such thing as objectivity. There is only subjectivity. That's the whole basis of the Heisenberg principle. There are not measurables in Reality. In quantum reality, there's only observables. You can witness certain things, but you can't measure them, because the minute you try to measure it, it already changes. You can't measure the same thing twice in quantum mechanics. One observation totally changes it. When you go back, it isn't there anymore.

That opens, then, for us, that we can see, that spiritual work is very, very powerful, because it is the subjective reality out of which observables, supposed reality, arises in the first place.

It's encouraging to realize that your spiritual work is very, very powerful. The spiritual work that you do is very, very powerful.

People say, "How can I get from 150 to 200?" Well, you just follow, "be kind to your neighbor." So, here we have infinite, infinite power [Quantum side]. How much power is available in the quantum potentiality is infinite. Infinite. Infinite. Without beginning, without end, without limitation, without design or form.

Consequently, power is infinitely powerful.

—

CHAPTER 4

ONE'S LIFE CAN BECOME A MEDITATION

Ohm is something else. And the sound of *ohm* is inherent in all sound and can be heard by anybody who attunes to it, and you can hear it within your own mind, and it's the sound of the universe. Hmmm is there at all times. Hmmmm is there at all times. Ah-h men-n-n.

We know with that practice of Dr. Diamond, where you pound the thymus gland, and you go "hahaha" and you think of someone you love. And that instantly raises your energy and your vibration. And if you were in an energy field, it now puts you in a positive one. And it has an effect on the immune system. And of course, on the acupuncture system and on kinesiologic response.

So, now we've tried to create a context of rationality, not necessarily, but because the ego is a doubting Thomas, and in fact the ego is built on nothing but doubt; because of its doubt, we've tried to build a logical premise upon which one can approach spiritual reality, and at the same time be logical, scientific, modern, advanced, and educated. Anybody argues about it, you say, you don't know much about quantum mechanics, do you? The mere belief that prayer is effective is sufficient to make prayer effective, is it not? Even if prayer wasn't effective, the fact we all believe it's effective, it now *is* effective, I'll tell you; so that quantum potentiality then has no limitation, and therefore the degree of one's faith then empowers it. This group here is enormously powerful.

What it holds in mind rings out throughout of all of human consciousness.

So, we all serve all of life through all of our spiritual endeavors. Everything that we surrender to God, for the good of all, every advance, every forgiveness that we personally do, every time we let go of feeling sad and unhappy, and every negativity we let go benefits all of mankind. Consequently, anybody who is in spiritual endeavor is of service to man at all times, just by their intention.

So, meditation then is really changing the context of one's life. That one's life becomes a meditation, in that it's lived in form, but in the context of the awareness that divinity is the Unmanifest out of which the manifest is arising and you're merely witnessing creation unfolding in the world of form as it appears to perception.

* * *

So, people ask, you know, how can they advance their consciousness. In a way, I wish I had never calibrated all the levels of consciousness because people miss the point of it. The point of it is merely to show where one is on a pathway.

Consciousness is evolving. Where is it at a certain point? Well, of course it is amazingly instructive to calibrate a great many things. It gives you a comprehension of the evolution of consciousness from the beginning of time as it first manifests on this planet, in the forms of creation as it evolves up through the expressions of life, how it evolves through the primate and takes its expression in the form of the human brain, *Homo erectus* and now *Homo sapiens*, and in the book, we announce the birth of a new genus of man, *Homo spiritus*. The nature of man has actually shifted. In the late 1980s when the consciousness level of mankind went from 190, which is non-integrous and non-truth, and it jumped to 207. That was the beginning of a new paradigm. A new paradigm of what it means to be human.

One could be as a Saracen, as a Hun, one could be called human, calibrating at 110, slaughtering everybody. The only thing that primitive man thought about was slaughtering others.

And then looting and raping, and then slaughtering some more. If they had nobody to slaughter, they got bored, and they sailed around looking for somebody to slaughter. That's all they did. Europe, era after era, wasn't it? Century after century, it was this horde from here, this horde from here. I mean, these people had nothing to do. What did they do, sit around, and say, "Hey, let's go raid somebody?" So, we call that human. Well, it's really sort of prehuman, isn't it? It's human in an anatomical kind of definition. It's not human in what we mean by human. Human, by what we mean as human, to be human means to be aware of the impact of what you're doing on others. It's the beginning of spiritual awareness.

Then, in the late eighties, suddenly we see the consciousness of man jump to 207, in which spiritual awareness as an innate human quality comes into full recognition. You see, in the evolutionary tree, the primate-Neanderthal man doesn't evolve to *Homo erectus* into *Homo sapiens*. What happens is on the hominid tree, this branch goes off and becomes that. And this [other] branch breaks off. It's a new branch. It's not the evolution. The Neanderthal doesn't become President Bush, huh? Neanderthal goes this far, and Cro-Magnon comes out, see. And then, you know all the names. They're always finding some fossil somewhere. Creep-down man, or something. No, Piltdown man or Cro-Magnon man. So, the thing evolutionary-wise that's interesting is that they are different branches off the tree. It's not the original branch, see? The mouse does not become the lion, no. The mouse goes off this way, and the rat comes off this way, and then the marsupial goes off this way.

So, I think what's happened now is that the evolution of human consciousness is such that the human nervous system can now handle the energy required for spiritual awareness. I don't think lower entities, I don't think their nervous system is able to handle it. We never asked these things before. Let's ask, just for fun: "The nervous system of Neanderthal man is equipped to handle spiritual awareness—resist." (Not true.) He can't handle it. "So, what's happening now is actually through evolution, through evolution, the nervous system is able to handle spiritual energy—resist." (True.) "In this lifetime, it's been extremely, agonizingly, painful—resist." (True.) It's been extremely, agonizingly painful. Because each sudden, sometimes extremely major, advance in consciousness was also accompanied by a severe, burning, painful sensation throughout the human body. "That's what went on the other day—resist." (True.) Yeah, it just never stops. So, it's like the nervous system is evolving to handle . . . the spiritual energy is quite demanding. Jesus Christ sweat blood, you know. The Buddha was tormented by agony. Like his bones were all broken, beset by negative energies, etc. But he said his bones were all broken. And we read that in Korea, and instantly it was okay that that pain and agony would come and go. Okay for the Buddha, it's okay for me. Ha!

So, what's happening, then, is that the nervous system is evolving to be able to handle higher spiritual energies. If they're not that well-evolved yet, they're painful. Neanderthal man would have been miserable. I wanted to ask personally because the witness of personal experiences. . . . Let's see how we can ask this: "So, for mankind to evolve more spiritually, his nervous system actually has to evolve to be able to handle it—resist." (True.) His actual nervous system. Let's see. Is it the neurons? "It's the neurons themselves that have to evolve—resist." (True.) It's still not clear to me what causes the actual pain of it.

So, then, what's going on is that through evolution, then. . . . Evolution is the way creation appears on the planet. The nervous system of mankind is evolving so as to be able to handle the enormous power of a higher spiritual energy. If you're not ready for it, it's really quite painful. It's really quite agonizing. And when you clear up some spiritual dilemma, at least in my experience, some major spiritual dilemma, there would be a whole period of feeling like all your nerves were on fire. I mean, it's just horrible, really. But the realization of what's the cause of it makes it bearable. So, it means to me that evolution now is that mankind's consciousness level is rising. His nervous system has to rise in order to be able to handle it. He has to evolve in order to be able to handle a higher spiritual energy.

We share our spiritual strength and hope with each other because through that mutuality we create a field, and the field itself tends to support the advancement of consciousness. The teacher, the energy field of the teacher, is one of context. Out of the context arises content, which the audience finds interesting. But it's really the context that gives the content its meaningfulness, its comprehensibleness, its impact. It helps people accept things that they find unacceptable.

Understanding Muscle Testing

There's always questions about the technique of kinesiology, and I can't really go into it. We've done it many, many times. We'll go through it one more time. We'll do it one more time—the basics of what you need to know, Susie and I. Come on over here in the light, Susie. You see, the two people have to be integrous. You've got to calibrate over 200. It means your intention has to be that you're interested in the truth for the sake of truth, you know what I'm saying? It's like an innate curiosity about what is the truth of this, you know, what is the truth of something? So, you have an innate curiosity about what is the truth of a thing, not for some reward, not for sensation, not because you can win in the stock market, you know. You have to really, really want to know what is the truth of this matter. So, the two people are integrous. They don't have any background noise; they don't have any music; they don't have any distractions. Their intention is to come together to discern the truth. We've found in experience which one of us serves as the best—I'm good for the questioning; she's good at answering. So, you find a person you can work with. Now, the question itself, the intention of the question, has to be integrous.

So, two integrous people come together. They want to know for the sake of truth and the pursuit of truth, you know, what are the facts about the case? And they then simply ask with two fingers, and they press down, and I say, "Resist." That's all she does is resist. You know, you don't have to be a rocket scientist to do kinesiology. Some people make it so difficult.

Now there's a comparative difference of the strength. I don't bear down as hard as I can to see if I can break her arm down: "What I'm holding in mind is true—resist." (True.) I can do it with one finger. So, she resists to the degree that it takes to resist one finger. All right. Now, if I ask another question, and the same amount of resistance doesn't hold her, then she goes down. So, when she resists, she resists to the same amount of strength, let's say. How much strength does it take to resist one finger? Next time I ask a question, she's going to resist to that extent because we want to compare the two, you understand? We're trying to compare two states of strength. So, if this time she resists lightly and next time she resists mightily, she's going to throw off the answer. So, the person, if you use common sense, what you're trying to do is just . . . you're trying to get a comparison between the two states. That's all we have to do, so it's very, very simple. It's yes or no.

So, when I used to do it in front of large audiences—we had a thousand people—we'd divide up into 500 pairs of doctor and patient. And I would hold up an apple and I'd say, "Okay, everybody in the audience, doctors get ready, test the patient." Okay. "Now look at this apple up here." Okay. "Now resist." And then I'd say, "All right. Now look at this apple." Then they would resist. "Resist." Okay. They would look at this apple, but on that apple, they would all go weak. This was a thousand people I'd never met—I didn't know any of them. Five hundred couples of doctor and patient. When they looked at this apple, they all went weak. When they all looked at this [other] apple, they all went strong. One had pesticide in it, the other didn't. That's all there was.

We repeated the same thing in Korea. Dr. Moon handed us two bags with green leaves in it. We didn't know what it was even about. She said, "Test these out." One made everybody go weak. One made everybody go strong. Then she opened it up later and said one had a pesticide in it. So, that's all there is to the kinesiologic test. It's not really difficult. If people get different answers, there's a number of reasons. One is the shift of intention. You can have background music; you can have things throwing you off. We sometimes find that husbands and wives don't work well together.

I don't know why. But not infrequently we'll get a married couple say, "For some reason we can't seem to work with each other." I suppose if we spend enough time with kinesiologic research, we could find why that is so in that specific pair. We did find a reason— something about chi energy. Oh, yes. We found that some people really couldn't do kinesiology. It had to do somehow with the balance of the chi energy in their acupuncture energy system, their energy system.

We never did really find out why a lot of people can't do it other than non-integrity: "Some people are not really capable of it because of the chi balance in their energy field—resist." (True.) Yeah, we get a yes to that. Of the people in this room, for instance, what percent would have that problem? "We have permission to ask that—resist." (True.) "More than five percent might have that problem." (Not true.) "More than four percent might have that problem." (Not true.) Oh, that's because of the people in this room. In the public. "In the public, more than five percent." (True.) "Ten percent." (True.) "Fifteen percent." (Not true.) Yeah, so in the public, just the public at large, probably, something about the imbalance of their chi energy. They're not suitable.

I just wanted to answer that question about kinesiology because you can't go into the details. And you have to find somebody that you can work with.

We were talking about how to forgive yourself out in the courtyard before, and we were joking around. If you're rotten and no good, so you're rotten and no good. So? What's to forgive yourself for? That you're wicked and bad? Of course, you're wicked and bad. We're all wicked and bad, man, or we wouldn't be here, right? You're rotten, no good, and it was a terrible and awful thing to do. So, we unplug the guilt because guilt, like we were saying before, guilt is its own payoff. If it's okay to feel guilty and okay to be wrong, and okay, then there's no payoff and that disappears it. How long can you hang on to guilt if it's okay to be rotten and no good? Everybody here's rotten and no good, right? What would a lifetime be if you weren't rotten and no good? You wouldn't have to be here. I mean, a whole lifetime is spent overcoming being rotten and no good, worthless, wrong, stupid; and if not, endeavors to prove that the other guy is. If we're not, then he is. So, that's the game, huh?

We're going to do a lot of teachers in the book. Some of these teachers I don't know. People find obscure writers elsewhere that I've never heard of. I don't know. All the truth that's ever been needed has already been written, you know. You don't have to look through the back stacks in the bookstore to find Hocus-pocus that lived in 1412 and what he said. I mean, it's interesting what he said, and it may or may not be true. And I can understand that one would want to know. But we can ask this one. I don't know who he is, but it probably wouldn't be valid. No, I don't think it would be valid.

* * *

Is discovering the unmanifest a function of exact focusing or peripheral focus? Seeing the unmanifest, seeing that which is non-form in form, it is far more advanced. You start out by realizing that that which you are is the context out of which all of life in all of its expressions both subjective and supposedly objective is arising. That you are the field out of which that is all arising. It starts out as the visual field. All that's happening within this room is happening within an infinite space of silence and non-form, out of which arises sound and all those things.

Is there such a thing as individual identity? There is, as far as imagination goes, as far as the ego goes, that which is karmically inheritable from one thing to the next is the degree to which one holds one's identity of self with the ego. It's illusion; it's transitory. It lasts of course for hundreds of millions or thousands of years. So, eventually it wears out, but the thought that "I am this" or "I am that" within form then creates a karmic consequence. The thought that I am an individual separate from God, that I am that which is born and dies, that I am that which calls itself "me," this physicality and its history—yes, they all have karmic consequences. That's what the Buddha meant when the Buddha said if you don't want to keep reincarnating, then you've got to become enlightened and transcend and realize that you are that out of which—you are that out of which that formulation arises. You are not the formulation; you're that out of which the formulation arises. You're not the thought. You're that out of which the thought arises. You're not the emotion. You're the source out of which that emotion arises. To realize that you are *a priori* to mind.

So, in meditation, then, one witnesses the procession and by one-pointedness of mind one, all of a sudden in one instant gets that I am that out of which thought arises. You realize that mind, that mind, speaking generically, is that which is present just prior to thought. The field, the field here. You don't know thought until you hear it from me. What was there right prior to my saying that? You understand? There's a readiness, a presence, the capacity for awareness, the capacity of hearingness, the capacity for comprehension-ness, is already here—it's already in existence before I just said that. Got it? Right before I said it, you're what you are before I say anything. How do I know what it's going to do? It just jumps across the stage and does anything it wants to. It does anything it wants to. Thank goodness, it obeys the law, or it would get arrested. Thank goodness it's been trained, to at least have a radar unit in the car. Ah, yes. That radar unit tells you what's coming up ahead of time, huh? A little anticipatory preparation. And that's what the mind is doing, you see? Like a little radar unit. It isn't there on your screen yet, so you're the screen that has the capacity to register the thought as it's said. It's very simple to realize that you're the unmanifest out of which the manifest arises.

The translation of the Buddha, then, is out of the unmanifest, the potentiality to realize that you are the source of the manifest out of which comes existence, out of which comes beingness, I am-ness. The book I'm finishing now is called "*I*," not "I am-ness." "Am-ness" is already late in the game. Don't you understand? "I" is prior to "am-ness," prior to existence. That which I was prior to this little body suddenly appearing in this wagon, trauma day. The infinite potentiality for that consciousness to arise and then presume existence, yeah, because it identified with the physicality, then it went into shock about existence versus non-existence.

The unmanifest is prior to beingness, prior to existence, prior to "is-ness," prior to "am-ness." Prior to "am-ness," prior to "is-ness," prior to existence. Prior to consciousness itself. Nisargadatta said that, didn't he? Yeah, he was right. First time I read that, I said, "What the hell does that mean?" It's just that it's so obvious.

Just know that you are the field out of which arises the content of the field, because how do you know there's anything in the field? You can only know by knowing it. That which has the capacity of knowingness has the capacity for recognition, see. You see, it goes back then to that's what meditation is. So, contemplation, then, is walking about in the world in a meditative state in which one's focus is on the source out of which the entire phenomena is arising. Outside of time, outside of conceptualization, outside of worryingness, outside of giving it names. There's awareness of awareness, but there's no awareness of an "I" being aware. That's a mentation that you add on top of it.

What Is the Essence of Renunciation

Renunciation is one of the traditional pathways to God. It's very often associated with meditation as a formal discipline. One renounces the world, joins a monastery, lives a certain kind of a life. And a lot of spiritual seekers sort of feel guilty that they're not doing that. You know, periodically, you think, "You know, if I were really spiritually committed, I wouldn't be driving on the way to work here; I'd be, you know, eating rice and beating on gongs and meditating, shave my head and sitting still and not fooling around here in the world." So, a lot of us go through that period of feeling guilty that we have not, you know, reached the maximum extreme of renunciation.

I want to talk about renunciation, what is the essence of renunciation, because in a way, all spiritual work is renunciation. For one thing, you're renouncing the negative for the positive. So, all spiritual work is in essence, renunciation.

Let's ask about the calibration level of consciousness of mankind: "We have permission to ask that." (True.) "The consciousness level of mankind, all of it, the world population is over 207." (True.) "208." (Not true.) "It's at 207." (True.) "208." (Not true.) No, still 207. The consciousness level of mankind doesn't move for long centuries. I don't know why. It stood at 190 for many, many centuries. If you go back to the 1500s, 1400s, it stood at 190. Many, many centuries. And then suddenly, quickly jumped to 207, and now because somebody asked has it moved, it's still at 207.

What does that mean? It means whatever you want it to mean. Nothing in and of itself has any meaning, you understand that. All meaning is a projection, an interpretation, a superimposition. If you look at a sunset, what does it mean? It doesn't mean anything. It is what it is as the expression of the divinity of its expression of its essence. Nothing means anything; therefore, nothing has a "why" to it. Why is a sunset? What do you mean, why is a sunset? It just is, huh? The mind is not happy with that; it wants an explanation for things because it wants to propagate itself. If it can formulate a question, then it justifies another large research grant, for one thing! It does it; it just *is* that way, you know. It just *is* that way. Like that fuzzy little thing on the microphone. I mean it just is what it is, you know what I'm saying? I'm sure people have explanations for it, but whatever it was, I thought it was adorable. Sort of miss it now, actually.

We wanted to sort of add to the discussion of meditation, some commentary on attachment and renunciation. What the mind has trouble letting go of are its attachments. We talked about that this morning. One attachment is the emotional payoff. Another attachment to thoughts is the narcissistic investment— the thought that *I created those thoughts; they're mine; they're precious.* The over-valuation of thoughts because of our own—of the narcissism that is innate to the ego. As we mentioned before, how the ego arises, its origination in this domain, in this dimension, now this planet, you know, it arose as an evolutionary outgrowth of animal, the animal nature. So, there's no point in feeling guilty about your ego and how it operates. It grew over the millennia. Millions of years of evolution. The animal has to know "here" from "there." And it presumes the reality of a "here" and "there," and for survival, therefore the ego is based on a duality of "this" versus "that." Good to eat, not good to eat. Friend/foe. It gets into dualities of opposites. In the animal world, that's very useful. You better know what's to eat or what's gonna eat you. You better know the difference, and if you're going to jump on a mouse, you'd better know that you are "here" and the mouse is "there," so that you can estimate the jump. So, the whole ego, then, is based on the animal consciousness of survival. So, it's basically dualistic by virtue of its structure. Because it's structured that way, there's no point to feeling guilty about it because you didn't create it that way. It thinks in terms of good/bad, right/wrong, et cetera.

With the development of forebrain, the intellect now, the style of animal instinctual expression takes on far more elaborate form. Far more elaborations now. So that what were limited to the physical reach of the animal can now be extended out globally via the Internet. What was once limited to the edge of the woods can now threaten the whole universe, the whole world, the human world. So, we see the intellect then extended animal motivations and contextualizations about reality and have spread them out into much more sophisticated extensions. Intrinsically, however, they are still the same thing.

The animal, in order to survive, then, valued certain things, and there arose attachment. And attachment really begins, you might say, noticeably in the mammalian world. The infant's attachment to the mother is essential and critical to survival. Emotional attachment—we see the beginning, then, of that which is nurturing in the evolution of the animal world that wasn't there with the dinosaur. It shows up in the bird. The mother bird hangs around, waits for the little birdies, and feeds them. And then we see the development, really, through the maternal bond, the development of love, which later develops into romantic love between male and female. But love really first emerges within the animal kingdom as maternal nurturance. So, attachment then comes in very early. The infant is obviously quite attached. It gets attached to the mother. It's actually the mother's lovingness to which the infant owes its survival. The mother's lovingness is a nonlinear reality. The mother's physicality is linear. The infant doesn't differentiate the two. It gets that love and survival are coming from "this" and gets attached to that physicality and that form. It isn't "this" that's ensuring the infant's happiness and survival, but the lovingness which is not physical. So, its physical survival is really based on the nonlinear. Its linear survival is really coming as a result of the nonlinear because love, which calibrates at 500, and unconditional love at 540, love, lovingness, is what is the source of the infant's survival, which then takes expression through the mother's nurturance. Anyway, attachment then becomes a habit. Attachment is also, because we identify with what we consider to be our own narcissistic creations, our own thoughts and feelings, and they become overvalued.

Traditionally, one could renounce the world and join a spiritual organization. That is time-honored. It is recognized throughout society to join a monastery, to join a nunnery. To renounce the world is a traditional pathway to God, in which one acts out, you know, in the external world and makes an absolute statement and leaves the world. So, traditionally at one time, most serious spiritual seekers, or many, were actually renunciates. One could become a hermit. One could become solitary. One could join a small group, or one could join a large organization, and become a formal renunciate.

The use of the word *renunciation* was of the materiality of the world, acquisition, ownership, and therefore the historical attributes of the renunciate was poverty, patience, sexual abstinence, and devoting one's life to service for others. In the meditative tradition, then, it allowed for a great deal of time and energy to be devoted to meditative practice itself. Meditative practice itself works out well. At the same time, I notice experientially with manual work, one meditates to the point of almost nonreality of the physical body, and you forget to eat and all that. And you stay sort of grounded, they call it, by doing physical work. There doesn't seem to be any conflict between physical work and meditation. One can continue right on with physical, manual labor and not interrupt the meditation at all. You go right on digging a ditch, and it doesn't seem to interfere with anything. So, the tradition of monastic life of prayer and meditation and simple manual labor, which is traditional, seems to work out quite well. Traditional, let's say, meditative practice and intellectualism dealing in the world of form and commerce is much more difficult to do. It's not that it's impossible, but it's difficult to look over a corporation's corporate accounts and at the same time, be in a really cool state, yeah?

So, there is gross renunciation as a lifestyle, as a major commitment, and many people here have done it in previous lifetimes, and some will probably do it in future lifetimes. And, in many people it is a part-time thing. For many people in the room here who have semi-normal lives, there are periods where you go on retreats. There are many hours during the week that you spend on meditation. So, you try to do a balance between handling the world and at the same time progressing spiritually. The progression spiritually through meditation has classically been likened to renunciation. In this case, the renunciation is mental rather than a social lifestyle. So that all spiritual work, in a way, is a renunciation.

First of all, we've talked in previous talks about transcending the opposites. The polarity of the opposites is an illusion, and one doesn't have to choose between opposites. One merely sees what seems like the opposite direction as an alternate. One then refuses the alternate and merely chooses the positive. So, you don't have to be against what is seen to be the negative. You don't have to hate sin and get out there and fight sin, you just choose virtue, right? So, you choose the positive rather than attacking the negative, so as to avoid getting polarized between the good and bad, good and evil, up and down, and all those illusions.

So, renunciation in its essence then, not as a lifestyle, but as an essence is the essence of all spiritual work, because you're at all times renouncing it as an attachment, renouncing it as a value, renouncing it as a way that you choose to go. So, by choosing the positive, in a way, you're always renouncing the negative, you know. To renounce allowing a certain thing to dominate your consciousness.

* * *

How do you handle anger? You see, that will bring up then what is the anger about, and you'll see to let it go will require a relinquishment. So, the relinquishment could be semantically referred to as a renunciation. The anger, then, is about a positionality. The willingness to let the positionality go is a renunciation. It's a renunciation of the payoff of the emotionality that goes with it, for one thing.

Those who have done the *Course in Miracles* remember, you know, that anger would come from perception. Perception comes from illusion, and by the willingness to surrender it to the Holy Spirit, you're asking God to recontextualize how you're seeing it, to replace perception with spiritual vision. And what does that mean? It means to see it minus dualistic illusion.

The pathway to God, we sort of represent in all the lectures, you know, is really the pathway of devotion; devotion is underneath it, but it seems to be the pathway through mind. It's really actually the pathway through no-mind. Well, we talked about the unmanifest as the ultimate, we'll talk about no-mind, right? Because once you start talking about mind, you're talking about form. So, all forms of meditation in spiritual work are, in essence, a renunciation. It's a rejection of what seems to be "this" direction for "this" direction. It's choosing the positive rather than anything else.

That always means letting go of the attachment, and the attachment then means the imaginary value. So, anger would be, then, hanging on to the imaginary value of a certain positionality. Renunciation would be the willingness to let go of that seeming benefit. Then what happens is the field of consciousness itself recontextualizes, and you see it differently; and now because you see it differently, there's nothing to be angry about. Does that answer the anger problem? But it represents how in meditation one looks at, one dissects and disassembles the construction that leads to the anger. So, meditation, in a way, is a constant deepening. It's a deconstruction of the formulation of what appeared to be a problem. As you take it apart, it disappears as an illusion, and there's nothing to handle because it has no reality.

* * *

What is the free will in a divinely unfolding universe? The question of free will is a whole other question. We said that everything is happening of its own, including the appearance of the human ego. As we said, the ego arises out of the evolution of consciousness, beginning in the animal world and evolving up to humanness, in which conflict doesn't even begin to arise in any kind of a serious manner until the physical consciousness, the consciousness of physicality, begins to meet spiritual reality. That's where *Homo spiritus* is born. The animal doesn't have any conflict, does it? It doesn't have a spiritual nature that has to balance against its animal nature. In fact, up to level 200 (somebody was asking me about that), up to level 200, it's not a real problem. Below that you just hate people, and you enjoy hating them, and you don't have any problem about that. They're American, so you kill them, what's the problem? Let's ask about that: "We have permission to ask the question—resist." (True.) Let's see. Below 200 is below integrity—resist. "Below 200 is below integrity—resist." (True.) "That which is non-integrous is denied the power of truth— resist." (True.) Oh, I see. So, you see, as you go up the levels of consciousness, power increases. So, you don't give gunpowder to children, right? Understand? It's only as you become purified now that you're given a new tool that's enormously powerful.

You realize the capacity to be able to tell the truth from falsehood about anything, anywhere in time or the universe has never existed in human history. It just got born: "That's why *Homo spiritus* is getting born—resist." (True.) Wow! "*Homo spiritus* really began in the late 1980s—resist." WOW! See, we find out things all the time. They come to your mind, you say, "I just gotta know that." People want to know how kinesiology works. That's how it works, you see. And if you've got time, the two of us can get into it, you know, when you start researching a thing, and that brings up the next question, and that brings up the next question. Oh, yeah. So, *Homo spiritus* is newly born, marked by what I call the antecedent of the second coming of Christ: "The second coming of Christ would really be preceded by 'shuuuuu'—resist." (True.) "That 'shuuuuu' began in the 1980s—resist." [True] "That 'shuuu' meant 207." (True.) That's the second coming of Christ, see. Like the dawn arising, you know, you don't go from black to suddenly Jesus Christ is standing there blasting everybody away and they are all going, "Wow." It's like the energy begins to arise so that he would make sense to you. It makes sense to you. Does Jesus Christ make sense to the monkey island at the zoo? No. He could stand there and preach all day, it wouldn't mean anything, right?

Consciousness has to . . . so, it's like a preparatory advancing of consciousness that's able to handle the truth. The human nervous system has to evolve to be able to handle it.

So, the evolution of consciousness, then, means that the stage is being set, that profession of consciousness is evolving. It evolves, and as it evolves, now it's crossed over to a different paradigm of reality. I was calibrating Walmart. You know, Walmart recently has become the largest corporation in the world. When I did research on Walmart, and I corresponded with Sam Walton and I admired his integrity, and he was a man who was putting integrity into the business place. I mean, that was revolutionary. And what would come of that? Well, in those days Walmart calibrated in the high 300s. It still does. So, integrity resulted in its becoming the greatest corporation in the world. I think that's just an interesting phenomenon, because here we're in an era where consciousness is for the first time in human history jumping from non-integrity to integrity, and then we have a demonstration of it in the marketplace. Well, spiritual terminology is not meaningful to large numbers of the population. Certainly, the bottom line of the biggest corporation in the world is very meaningful to a lot of people.

And the *Wall Street Journal* called me up a couple of months ago and wanted to know how real is that. How real is it that if you put spiritual reality into the business world, that it literally shows up in the bottom line? Well, I think Walmart answered that question, didn't it? Just like Enron or WorldCom answered the other direction. For things to survive now, it seems to me, they will have to become integrous. In a non-integrous world, integrity is not required to survive, at all. You can succeed in a non-integrous world by stealing everybody else blind and threatening them with guns and invasion. In a more integrous world, this doesn't work anymore.

So, what we've seen I think, is a new dimension of the prevalence of human consciousness. Its energy level rises and with it, it lifts all of mankind. What was okay before, because it was above the line, is now below the lines. So, as the water rose, that which was above the water is now below the water. And I think what will be acceptable, and what will prevail in mankind is going to shift as a result of the consequence of the energy field itself. So, we saw this morning how the energy field itself lifts and sustains in an impersonal, non-linear way just by the nature of its gravity. So, the human, then, is like a cork in the field of consciousness. And what accounts for the evolution of one's individual consciousness is letting go of ballast. As you let go of ballast, your cork automatically rises. The field doesn't move. Although we said the prevailing field on the planet now at 207 is quite a bit different than 190. They're two different dimensions of existence altogether.

I think we've answered those questions. We see that renunciation, then, is a lifestyle. Renunciation can be best expressed as its corollary—not its opposite, but its corollary, which is the choosing of the positive. It's not necessary to renounce the negative, but only to choose the positive and bypass the polarization. Bypass getting stuck in a positionality.

Q: "Where does emotion fit in spiritual growth or spiritual values? It seems that every time it's spoken of, they're not serving the spiritual life well."

We see on the Scale of Consciousness that the emotion depends on the level of integrity and that emotion itself is not necessarily detrimental. We were talking about negative emotions which calibrate below 200: hatred, anger, self-pity, guilt, remorse. But as you get over 200, now emotion becomes a positive asset. The commitment to integrity is a certain emotionality. It's not emotionality the way most people think of it, but it's a certain space of commitment. You can do it when you clean up the kitchen in the morning. You can commit to getting this place absolutely clean the way I want it. Eventually you see as the emotion goes up, it calibrates higher and higher. Probably the most important emotion—and we will get to that in a later lecture—in spiritual work is that of love, but beyond that, devotion.

What makes any spiritual understanding comprehensible, and work, is one's devotion to the truth. So, the pathway of heart and pathway of mind are one and the same. They end up one and the same. Because the pathway of Advaita, let's say, Advaita, pathway of No-mind, the pathway of Zen, is really based on a profound and intense dedication. One-pointedness of mind is the expression of an intense dedication, a love that is not in the world of ordinary emotionality. The love, the devotion to achieve one-pointedness of mind, is extreme and intense. To leave everything in the world, fixate only on that which is straight ahead of you, with no deviance, takes an intense dedication, and that is devotion.

There's a very simple way to meditate, and one that I teach people most generally, is to merely sit and close your eyes. If you sit and close your eyes and look straight ahead, you'll see little corpuscles. If we all look ahead—close your eyes and look ahead, you see all little dancing corpuscles, right? Those are little blood corpuscles going through the capillaries in the retina. And you just look straight ahead. If you look straight ahead, you see there's no real form there; there's all these little dancing, little particulates of light. Little illuminations, like. If you look straight ahead, then you see this sort of a semi-blank field of little dancing, miniscule, tiny dotlets of light. One can just look at them observationally without comment or anything. And at the same time, be aware of one's breathing. Not to alter it, just be aware of the breathing. So, within oneself, you're watching the breathing and you're looking straight ahead, and you just profoundly relax and let that take you wherever it takes you. As you do, the sense of being "me" here, begins to disappear. The sense of infinite space begins. One gets the feeling that it's almost like space looking at space, like there's not an individual person looking at the back of the eyelids. It's like it's beginning—it happens of its own. The breathingness also, one becomes aware is happening of its own. There is no breather doing the breathing. There is no thinker doing the thinking. There is no seer doing the seeing. No thinker behind the thoughts, no doer behind the actions. No looker, even. All this is just happening of its own, spontaneously.

Choose to Go in the Direction of God

Where does free will come in? Free will comes in, then, in choosing to go in the direction of God. Choosing to go in the direction of spiritual truth as one understands it at this point of the evolution of one's own consciousness. Free will, then, is the innate capacity for choice. But that choice is limited. It's karmically determined. The choices of the past have already determined the possible choices of the present. A zebra cannot choose to be a kangaroo. So, the karmic evolution of consciousness throughout all of the evolution of human consciousness and its expression in one's own particular karmic development, then, results in a certain range, a certain range of karmic possibilities. Within that range, free will operates to the degree that one energizes it, chooses it, wishes it. Free will doesn't mean that a camel can decide to be a kangaroo, no. Free will means that within the range of what is possible due to my own karmic inheritance, what is within the range of possibility, one can make the choice. However, the minute that choice is made, it already shifts the future choices. So, free will then makes a choice from moment to moment. Each choice then instantly changes the potentiality. It either enlarges the choice or decreases the choice. We saw that on our chart of quantum mechanics. Every choice then becomes, you might say, a chaos theory of bifurcation. So, free will is like an endless series of bifurcations. Because I choose this, now these possibilities open up. And again, if I choose this [other one], thereby, this whole basket of opportunities open up. Now, if I choose to be part of the field rather than the particular, I've immensely opened my potentialities. When you choose the field rather than the content of the field, now you're choosing an infinite potentiality.

So, a group like us here today, by commitment have chosen to realize the truth of one's reality as context. So, habitually, the members of the group here, in their own spiritual practice, are constantly bypassing content. And constantly opening the avenue for the conscious awareness of context as their ultimate reality. By saying, "I am not this, I am not that," the pathway of negation. Or by saying, "I am this, and I am that," one is already changing one's karmic potentiality. To go out of this body and come back in another, then, one starts with the basket of infinite potentialities that you left off with the last time, because you, frankly, wore out the last body. Why can't you keep one body for a hundred thousand years? Well, until you're done with evolution, it's because it doesn't work out that way.

I can't know what it is to be Black if I've got a white body. I don't know what it's like to be a woman if I've got a male body. I mean, I'm stuck with the limitation, you understand? So, you may choose to come back as everybody, sort of. Sort of the everythingness of potentiality. The only way you can know a thing is to be it. That's why. You can't know it by reading about it. I don't know what it is to be a woman, unless I *am* one. I can read about it. It's interesting, intriguing, and I can become very, very erudite about it, but I don't know what it is to be it unless I *am* it.

So, one thing that karmic evolution, one of its great values is you get to understand and know things by virtue of being them. So, those two lifetimes, I realize why I did them. Yeah. You have to actually *be* that to *get* it, to know what that is. Hmm. Wow. There's some rough lifetimes, but that's the only way you got to know it, you know.

See, the mind cannot know anything. It can only know *about* them something. It sounds like a fine distinction, but it's crucial. The mind can only know *about* a thing. The only way to *know* a thing is to *be* it. Be it. To be the context out of which all of seeming reality arises is the way you realize—that's what's called self-realization. To realize it by being it: "So, realization is just that recognition that you are it—resist." (True.) Ha! I always thought it was simple, right? The realization that one does realize the realization of what is real, is realization. That's a good example, you see what I'm saying?

The only way to realize what it is to be a human being is to be one, and then you *get* what it is. It's very difficult; it's very complex; it's very challenging. I think anybody who has lived a human life deserves to go to heaven. If I was St. Peter, I'd say, "You lived a human life; pass." Because its challenge is exquisite. You know, the complexity of the human mind itself. Its enormous identifications as consciousness evolved throughout time. Its enormous capacity for identification and then losing the reality of who it is in that identification, you know. It loses touch with that which it really is. It loses the fact that it's context, and it begins to believe that it's content. That's all that's happening. That's all that's happening is that it loses, you know, like Krishna. And he wanted to know what it was like to be a cow and became one, and then he forgot that he'd willed it. Some other god had to come and rescue him to remind him. He forgot that he'd willed himself to be a cow to see what it was like to be a cow. Of course, as a cow he didn't remember that he had willed it, because now he was a cow. Indra came and helped rescue him and said he'd wished himself to see what it's like to be a cow. So, we've done that as humans, haven't we? We've all been curious what it's like to be a human, and what it is to be here, and we've found out.

So, renunciation then is to renounce the false for the true, to see that truth has no opposite. There is no opposite to truth, just as there is no opposite to God. Only the true is true, and only that which exists has reality. Only the Allness of God has any reality. That takes care of existence versus non-existence. Allness versus Nothingness.

You know, how those karmic things persist in a lifetime. One time somebody went to a lecture that I gave back in Sedona Villa. That was, I don't know, back in the eighties, late seventies, somewhere. I was talking about the calibrated levels of consciousness in those days, and the part it played in sobriety and all. In the middle, this guy just went into a really great state. And after years of succumbing to alcohol, suddenly he was beyond it. In fact, I calibrated him one time. He went up 150 points. So, he came out of the pits and went into a state of, like, unconditional love and joy. So, anyway, a couple of months later, I hear a knock at the door and here he is. This guy's a workman and he's a very good carpenter, excellent carpenter, actually. And he backed up with a trailer, and here was this incredible table, made from a slab of wood this thick [about a foot], from the top of Mingus Mountain that had got hit by lightning in 1956, and he had saved this incredible slab of wood. And he made this incredible bench. I use it as a table. It weighs a couple hundred pounds. He spent six weeks making it, out of appreciation for his recovery. And he backed up this thing and somehow, we got it into the house. And there engraved on the top, in Sanskrit is, "Nothingness versus Allness." He'd never heard me; I'd never said anything about it. There at age three, "nothingness versus allness," and there it was inscribed and beautifully carved, Allness versus Nothingness.

So, you could see how karmically a thing like that prevails in the field of consciousness. It emerges, then, as getting reborn in another lifetime to transcend that illusion. Somebody picks it up, you know—in Sedona we call it "on the inner net." Somebody picks it on the "inner" net that's prevailing in your consciousness. And at the time he brought that, it was yet unresolved. Allness versus Nothingness was as yet not evolved in this consciousness. It was sometime after that. So, how did his psyche pick that up as the central theme of this lifetime? Because I didn't give lectures like I am now. I never mentioned anything about personal experience; I just talked about the calibrated levels of consciousness and all. So, somehow his psyche had picked up the central focus of that.

So, that's our karmic, you might say, our karmic unfoldment from lifetime to lifetime. And the choices we make, then, are the exercise of free will. Which for some reason, kinesiology as a tool is not suitable for somebody who calibrates below 200. In the beginning when I discovered that capacity of kinesiology to tell truth from falsehood, I didn't know what to do with it for years. And I didn't know whether to write about it, because at that time I thought it could be used for, you know, extremely nefarious ends, sort of like discovering gunpowder, you know, dynamite. Should you share that with the world or not? Discovering nuclear power, any of those things. Yeah, you know it's sort of a moral dilemma, so I really puzzled over it for years. Should this be shared with the world or not shared with the world, you know what I'm saying? At that time, I didn't realize that to make it work, you yourself have to be integrous, so it couldn't be used for non-integrity. But for years, I did not publish it or write about it because I thought at the time it was a double-edged sword and that it could be used to destroy mankind. And so, I didn't want to share it. And it was only later that I got that it was shareable and that it was safe, and that if your intention is less than 200 or the people are less than 200. In other words, it would be like non-integrous people can't make dynamite go off, so I was delighted to find that. I only found that out after I wrote *Power vs. Force*, and then I had to revise the new edition, because originally, I thought anybody could use kinesiology and get the truth about anything. And then later on I saw, hmm—oh, I know what resolved it. I saw that the only way you could get ahead would be by becoming more integrous. In other words, the only way you can, let's say, compete on the world of integrity is by becoming more integrous. The only way you can become more powerful is to become more loving. And therefore, it couldn't be used in a destructive way. And that understanding allowed me to publish *Power vs. Force*, but it was only after the first edition that I saw—we only lately discovered that unless you're over 200, and we didn't discover it until we started getting letters from people who said it didn't work. . . . Well, I'd used it for years in all kinds of groups and kinesiologists and holistic health practitioners. It always worked. It always worked, I never saw that it didn't work, so I thought, *Where is this coming from?* "Well, we tried it and it doesn't work." What do you mean it doesn't work? And then we discovered that it had these limitations, integrity of motive, integrity of intention, integrity of the two people. So, there was a built-in safeguard, because certainly to have the capacity to discern the truth or falsehood of anything gives you, in a way, an incredible degree of power.

Actually, the average person today, certainly anybody who attends these conferences, has more power than anybody who ever existed, really, in a way. Caesar didn't have the way to tell truth from falsehood, you know what I'm saying: "The average spiritually educated person now has more power than all the potentates who ever lived—resist." (True.) Yeah, you've got more power than Caesar ever had. Caesar couldn't tell the difference between truth and falsehood. You know? You can only go out there, and if you won, you were right, and if you lost, you lost. So, it's a gift that mankind has now. It's like a gift. It came out of that advancement of consciousness, so we were like given the gift of discernment. It was, throughout time, discernment was when the third eye opened up in the Buddhic body, and it didn't happen until you were quite evolved spiritually, to be able to look at a thing and see whether it's integrous or non-integrous, the true from the false, is a very advanced level of spiritual maturity, one which many people don't make; otherwise, all the false gurus and a lot of the New Age nonsense and circus acts would have no attraction.

When a person is very spiritually evolved, they see the essence of what a thing is just by glancing or just hearing about it. I can pick up a letter and I can tell you just by the feel of the letter what it's all about or what its energy is and ah, but it only comes at a certain point. Up to that time, you know, you're easily, easily bamboozled by all kinds of smoke and incense and sandals and long hair and oohs and aahs and mantras, and chants and music and gongs and bells and crap, you know. That's the astral circus in a way. And card readings and psychics and readings and Master This, That, and the Other on the other side that tells you to sell your Chevy and buy a Ford, okay.

So, the way to spiritual advancement is difficult. You have to evolve through the whole difficulty of being a human being, which in itself is quite a trip, is it not? Just to be a human being and survive is already an enormous confrontation, and it means, always it means in a certain way a constant renunciation, because the child, its first thing is to learn how to renounce "this" for "that." We call it "good" and "bad." So, the way the child, the normal child, works is its egocentricity is surrendered, because in return it gets approval and love from the mother. If you let go of this impulsivity and this greediness and this desirability, you get rewarded by approval from the mother. So, the evolution of a healthy human consciousness, then, really depends on adequate parenting.

If there's nobody there to reward you for letting go of your selfishness, then you end up a psychopath. And end up a sociopath. You just do what you want to do. If you want it, you steal it. If you take it and you feel like punching somebody, you punch him. So, the chronicity, the recidivism of criminality, is because at that critical level of human consciousness, there wasn't the letting go of the narcissistic core of the ego, which persists in the psychopath. There's really no point to incarceration, you know, as punishment is sort of idiotic. The reason it doesn't work is it has no reality to it at all. You know, because if this defect is a chronic illness, which it is—it shows up by age one or two or three—the inability to delay gratification, and then it shows itself as a pattern of behaviors which always ignores the rights and the feelings of others. It's just total egocentricity from the word *go*. This becomes a lifestyle, so putting somebody in prison for 18 years, it's not surprising that within 24 hours of letting him out, they do exactly the same thing that put them in prison the first time. It's because it's like an illness due to a defect, whether the defect is genetic or experiential because of lack of adequate mothering and parenting in childhood. But in dealing with it myself professionally, it seems to be an illness. Criminalism is an illness. Criminalism is an illness, and there's no treatment for it, except to protect society from it. You know, when you want to protect—if it's a ravenous predator, and you're not going to change his ways, there's no point in punishing the wolf for being a wolf. A wolf is a wolf. It's a predator. So, you can isolate yourself from the predator to protect society. So, you can put them in compounds where, you know, the fence down the middle, and predators on this side and non-predators on this side. That's what we do, don't we? We put the sheep on this side, and we put a fence between the wolf and the sheep, yeah? You don't punish the wolf for being a wolf. "Bad wolf, you ate sheep!" We'll give you 18 years. At the end of 18 years, what is the wolf going to do? It's going to eat the sheep first day out. After 18 years of not eating sheep, man you are really hungry for sheep.

In the most horrendous case of rape I've ever heard of—I don't want to even mention details, it was so awful. But this guy did something that was so horrible as to be unbelievable. And after 26 years in prison for doing this horrendous thing, you know, within 24 hours he did the same thing all over again to another woman. So, when you see that one of these recidivists are about to be released, you know the next crime is going to happen in the next 24 hours. So, we see criminalism, then, is a failure of this maturation process where you surrender the selfish egocentricity of the ego in return for love.

That devotion that is developed later, as the spiritually committed person has that to a high degree. That the sense of the absolute sovereignty of love as a central focus of one's life is what brings people to spirituality. Intuitive awareness that that which is infinitely loving is just beyond one's conscious grasp, and at the same time, is innate within one's presence as the reality of your own existence.

Creation . . . of course, religion has divided, you know, God into immanent and transcendent. And the mystic is the one in whom spiritual reality comes from within. To be faced with existence verses nonexistence does not come from without. It stems from the presence of God within you almost demanding recognition about its truth and its reality. The mystic, then, is the one who knows God as Immanent, as the Self. God Immanent as the Self. And in some religions, this is considered heresy, you understand. At one time I would have been burned at the stake. Was I ever burned at the stake? Probably. Anyway, I don't remember being burned at the stake; I think I do, yeah, oh yes. Anyway, being a mystic was not a good thing centuries ago in Europe. It would get you burned at the stake. The mystic did not fare too well in many civilizations, and it is today considered a heresy in many contexts. In Islam, for instance, the mystic is considered a heretic. See, Islam considers, talks about yoga: yoga, a union with God. It's like there's a "me" and then there's a "God," see. And then the two become like a unity. Well, inasmuch as there is only the sun shining, removing the clouds, the cloud doesn't join the sun, you see what I'm saying. That which is not real evaporates, leaving only that which is real, so there is no union of the unreal with the real. The ego doesn't join in a yoga and union with God, see. So, the mystic is a heretic in the views of Islam and in certain traditional branches of Christianity. It is not considered heretical in the Hindu or the Buddhist, but they're more sophisticated.

So, God as transcendent then means God as "otherness." You get the person looking for transcendent God, through religion, is looking for an "otherness," called "God." It's an "other." That's why the Buddha didn't talk about God because the minute you talk about God, you're looking for something other than what you are. There is me, wicked worm here, worthless worm, and then there's God. You see how separated that is? So, the more you insist on the reality of a transcendent God, the more you deny your own spiritual reality. If the only God that's a real God is transcendent, then your chances are nil, folks. Because his quality is different than yours.

The difficulties with the intellectual approaches to God is that let's say, let's take the arguments of Thomas Aquinas. When you go back through an endless series of causes to the prime cause, the epistemological error there is the failure to realize that the initial cause is a different quality than the rest of the billiard balls. An endless series of billiard balls does not start with one super billiard ball. It starts with one non-billiard ball. Oho! It changes its quality. As you go back to source, then you find a different quality than what you're looking for. You have to have something of a greater dimension. It's now in a different category of logic. You don't find the source of an endless series of billiard balls in one billiard ball. You find it in a non-billiard ball, huh?

So, most spiritual groups are made up of people who have gone a certain direction in religion. I love religion, and to this day adore it. I adore going to church. I adore the music. I adore the preaching. I love ministers and all that goes with the church. I love it. Except that's one direction to go and enlightenment is another. Salvation is one thing; enlightenment is another. Christ came for purposes of salvation. The Buddha came to teach enlightenment. Two different things.

Salvation from the illusion of your own reality. Karmically, we said that the universe is one karmic reality. The total universe is one karmic unity. In that karmic unity, there are the various levels and dimensions. And Christ said if you do things that calibrate below 200, you will end up next lifetime in very miserable places. So did Buddha say that. So did Krishna say that. Every enlightened being that's ever existed says there's a multi-strata, multi-strata within the realm of consciousness, going from the lowest hells to the higher hells, the purgatories, to lower heavens, to the higher heavens, to enlightenment itself, to go beyond all positionalities. They said don't go there; woe to those who abuse the innocence of the child because where they're going when they leave the body is not a pleasant place to go. So, Christ wasn't threatening you with hell, but he was telling you it's a fact that the karmic weight, the karmic calibration of one's karmic body, let's say, like a cork in the water will rise or sink to various levels. All I'm saying is the lower levels are incredibly awful. Having been there, I will guarantee you, I will tell you that hell is far worse than you can imagine. You can imagine the worst incredible hell in your imagination, and you are not even scratching it. And it goes far beyond that. It goes beyond the dreadful, beyond the terrible, beyond the indescribable, to realms of non-form. In the realms of non-form, hell takes on dimensions that you can't even imagine. And so, Jesus Christ, out of his love for mankind, he came down from heaven. He never had any previous lifetimes. He came down from heaven to tell you that that is the case, that if you choose below 200. . . . So, all Jesus said was, "Don't choose that which is below 200." That's all he said. If it makes you weak with kinesiology, bypass it. That's all Jesus said. Renounce that which is below 200. And that's all the Buddha said. That's all anybody's ever said.

We all know that the horrific leads us to intense inner psychic suffering. You don't have to be dead to discover hell. We've all done things that we've lain awake squirming with inner pain about, sometimes for months or years, even. So, you don't have to be dead to experience the consequence. So, everything has its own karmic corollary, not necessarily a consequence as though it was a punishment or something, but if you choose to walk within certain dimensions, you're going to be exposed to certain temperatures, barometric pressures, light radiations. The hells are very bad places to go. That's all Jesus says. Woe to those who do this, that, or the other, because you're going to experience hellish places.

Well, most people, because they identify with the body, don't remember the hells they're in. An enlightened person remembers it all. He'll tell you, not because he read it in a book, but because it's a recent experience. In this lifetime it's a very recent experience. I will tell you that hell is one hell of a valid place. It's possible to exist in a place of such spiritual pain and agony, one wishes that one had never come into existence at all. So, Jesus Christ told the truth. That was his purpose. The Buddha, when we ask about the Buddha, we get he had many, many lifetimes. Many, many lifetimes. And he said that the way out, the way out of it altogether is to transcend all identification with temporality and form. And then you will not be subject to reincarnated lifetimes, which may or may not be agonizing.

* * *

We said that prayer, when we were talking about quantum mechanics, we're trying to get the science of prayer, that prayer represents a potentiality. Opens a potentiality in the infinite reality. And is effective; again, its effectiveness has to do with the calibrated level of the prayer itself, the calibrated level of the person praying, that person's karma, and the karmic conditions of the world. So, how integrous is the prayer? Most prayers are like children's prayers. I can remember running for my violin lesson, praying up a storm. I left this little country school, and I gotta go one mile down Dean

Road and catch the bus. The buses were like every two hours, you know what I mean, not a bus every 10 minutes. So, it was *the* bus that would get you to your violin lesson. I'm carrying this violin case and I'm tearing down here one mile, going like hell, and praying up a storm the whole mile that God would hold up the bus till I got there, because I left five minutes late. The bus took off. No wonder I became an atheist for years, right. So, that's self-interest.

So, what is your expectation of prayer? That if you are presenting it as a gift to the universe, in that quantum potentiality, then you're influencing the likelihood. We said that quantum mechanics has to do with likelihoods and potentialities. The likelihood of your finding a thing where you saw it last time, is already changed—the Heisenberg principle. Heisenberg principle is that having looked at a thing, the likelihood that it's not going to be there the second time, because you've looked at it the first time. You've already changed the potential reality. So, prayer changes the potentiality. I think a thousand people praying for a certain thing increases the likelihood of that. It doesn't cause it, though, because reality is beyond cause, but it does increase likelihood. What I think it does is change the buoyancy of the cork, so the cork is more likely to rise up within the karmic reality of the sea. That's what I think prayer does, you know. Increases likelihood. It also creates form. It also creates form. Certainly, how did that carpenter know "Allness versus Nothingness" and do it in Sanskrit? I mean, how did he know that? He picked it up somewhere in form, you know. Any other question, and then we'll take a break, and then we'll just spend the rest of the day chatting.

Q: *"There are a lot of new spiritual masters, when you ask them about praying, they say that reinforces your delusion and your separateness from God. Can you talk about that and intention?"*

There are various different levels in which the question can be understood and answered. On a certain level, no prayer is necessary, nor is it answerable, nor does it have any reality. But that's one level. But that isn't the level that's meant by people when people say,

"How effective, how good is prayer?" I think prayer is as effective as one is karmically limited to at the time within a universe being what it is at the time. It certainly is a declaration of intention, certainly is a statement of intention. To say that prayer is saying that you're separate from God—you know, what is it that's praying? Your ego is what's praying. Your spirit doesn't need to pray. The ultimate reality of that which you already are is already there. There's no need to pray. So, it's the ego that's praying in the first place. The ego is not one and the same as God, or you wouldn't be a spiritual seeker. You would be approved, you'd be enlightened, you'd be a Christ. So, those are ways of constructing things. Any question can be addressed from different levels. So, one the values of the Scale of Consciousness is you can tell at what level do you want an answer because anything you can say about anything is only an appearance. It's only a style, a nominalization. Everything is, depending on from what position you're viewing it. Everything is a product of point of view. Any answer you can get is only an artificial construction coming out of a point of view. That's the whole basis of quantum mechanics. You find what you look for. If you're looking for dots and zeros, you'll find lots of dots and zeros. If you're looking for triangles and whistles, you'll find lots of triangles and whistles. That consciousness is of such a nature that it has an illusion; it thinks there's a "this" finding a "that." Actually, by asking "this," it's already defined the "thatness." The question itself has already defined the answer. Therefore, there isn't a "this" finding a "that." There's only consciousness coming to the obvious conclusion that whatever you ask about is what you're going to find. And certainly, quantum mechanics is a beautiful scientific way of stating what the Heisenberg principle is, you will discover what you're looking for. So, the advancing edge of physics is up against the fact that until it knows more about consciousness, it can't really make any further advance. Is it a "thisness" finding an objective about "thatness"? Or is it only discovering how the human mind works, projected out into an apparent universe, which an "illusory" thinks is a "that" being looked at by a "this"? No, it's all of "this" being looked at by a "this"; that's what we know from here. There's only a "this" finding a "this." And what it finds is—so, if you're looking for little blue pebbles, then you'll find little blue pebbles. And if you're looking for little green ones, you'll find little green ones, because that's what you are looking for. So, you can only discover that which you're seeking.

CHAPTER 5

—

SPIRITUAL INTENTION AND CHOICE

Q: *"To know something, to really Know, with a capital K, you have to actually be it. If Christ lived one lifetime, how could he have experienced so much?"*

Well, that I don't know. Our research merely was that Christ literally did come down from heaven to reveal the truth to mankind as most beneficially he was capable of knowing it at the time. I mean, Christ was born, you now, at a time and in a culture that determined what, to some extent, what he said. He, you know, didn't talk about karma specifically. He did mention that somebody or other, Elijah, was a reincarnation of John the Baptist. So, he did acknowledge in Thomas, the Gospel according to St. Thomas, that somebody was a reincarnation of a previously well-known person. From my own research, though, Jesus had never been prior a human being, never had a human embodiment, whereas the Buddha, in contrast, had had many.

So, they serve two different purposes, two different messages. You know, in general my understanding of Lotus Land Buddhism and Christianity is that the acknowledgment that the negativity of mankind is so prevalent that the likelihood of reaching enlightenment from this level is very slim. Now, I never calibrated what was the energy level of mankind at the time of Christ. We know it was at 190 for centuries. Let's see what it was at the time of

Christ's birth: "At the time Jesus was born, the consciousness level of mankind was less than 190—resist." (True.) "It was less than 180." (True.) "Less than 160." (True.) "Less than 140." (True.) "Less than 120." (True.) "Less than 100." (Not true.)

Consciousness level of mankind at the time of Christ's birth was only 100. What are you going to say to people who calibrate at 100—they sort of lived, you know—past history is all about greed, hatred, the guillotine, remorse, guilt, despair.

So he was born into tribal culture, which held to the belief in a sort of malevolent kind of gods. The gods of the Old Testament are prone to malevolence, anger, revenge, favoritism. In the midst of all that he's supposed to bring the message of heaven, the reality of God, the reachability of heaven, and what kind of behaviors will lead you in this direction, and what kind of behaviors will lead you in that direction. That there is the destiny of heaven and hell following the physical existence, so that was sort of a very basic message he gave. A very basic message. And at the time, even then, it was very revolutionary. He didn't speak of karma. I doubt very much it would have had any meaning at all to people in a culture like that.

* * *

The Buddha was born in a culture on the border of Nepal, you know, where the Aryan culture was already quite ancient. And the experience of the presence of God as the Self, to be enlightened, had already been a prior experience in that culture. So, in the culture in which the Buddha was born, the concept of karma was not novel or revolutionary. India has a far more ancient spiritual culture than the Western world and certainly the Islamic world. Other than that, I don't know, you'll have to ask him.

To experience the totality of the consciousness of mankind is what went on with Jesus Christ. To comprehend its downside, to sweat blood, in just looking at it, meant that he owned it as a totality, a totality of the energy field of what it is to be human, without necessarily experiencing it serially, you know. And karma would be the reincarnation, sort of reexperiencing what it means to be human, sort of serially. What's it like to be a slaver, what's it like to be a slave, what's it like to be each thing individually.

Q: *"Can you eat meat and achieve self-realization?"*

The question of vegetarian, which I haven't run into in a while, comes up periodically. The same with celibacy, the same with work, anything having to do with ordinary world. The person becomes spiritually aware or interested—first of all, they're going to start off at different levels. Somebody may start off at 100, some people may start off at 300, some people may start off at 400. So, the questions, each one is like a koan, like a Zen koan. What is the meaning? Well, if you see physicality as life and if life is limited to physicality, then being a vegetarian would certainly make sense. One doesn't want to kill anything in order to survive. So, at a certain level where you think the animal's dying and sacrificing itself for you, it would be wrong. Later on, you see the animal doesn't die anyway, and in fact, if you didn't eat it, it wouldn't even exist, and it doesn't even hardly notice going out of body.

Let's say, you're going to eat a steak, right? You say, "Poor cow, poor cow's gonna die because I eat the steak. You know, there wouldn't be any cattle out there if nobody ate steak. There wouldn't be any cattle. So, hundreds of millions of cattle would never know what it is to exist. It's only because you eat steak that they get to here, you understand what I'm saying? If nobody eats me, I wouldn't be here, would I? "We have permission to ask about the cattle—resist." (True.) "The cow notices it when he leaves it, when he leaves the physical and goes into the other domain—resist." (Not true.) He doesn't notice it. If you swat a fly, the fly just goes right on flying. He's in his astral body—etheric body—and he doesn't notice he's dead? He comes back. The witness would notice the difference, but the fly doesn't know there's a difference. When you go out of the body at death, all you notice is the physicality is laying there, but there's no discontinuity in the sense of self, no discontinuity. "There's no discontinuity in the sense of self at death—resist." (True.) That's correct. So, the cow doesn't even know that it just got eliminated from the physicality. "That is a fact." (True.) The cow doesn't know it. Goes on right along in its etheric body and has no interest in the whole deal. If you asked a more evolved cow. . . . I was in a high state one time, probably in the high 500s or somewhere. This is a statement of fact. "It is my joy to give up my physicality for Thee, O Lord." (True.) That's a fact. Out of choice, I do sacrifice my physicality for that which is higher than myself, and in so doing I join that which is divinity and share in that awareness.

So, by surrendering its physicality to a higher being, it supports the evolution of consciousness and karmically earns the right to that awareness itself. "We call that, within the animal kingdom— that exists as animal grace. Grace." (True.) That's the grace of the animal. You know what's meant by "animal grace"? Animal grace is apparent. You look at a deer and it stands there in its incredible grace, beauty, and magnificence because it is completely its own potentiality. It feels no tension between what it is and what it thinks it could be. It is already completely its potentiality. So, it has infinite serenity. You know, my cat as it sits there is in a Buddha state. It's still; it's completely what it is, with no anxiety or strain. It's called animal grace. "That is correct—resist." (True.)

So, the grace of the animal is that it is the completion of its karmic potentiality. It is itself the perfection of the fulfillment of the potentiality of its essence. And that's why it has the Buddha nature. Let's see: "The animal is at one with Buddha nature—resist." (True.) So, you don't have to worry about the animal. All right.

So, if you're at the point where you think that you're killing a life, it would be wrong to eat meat. When you see that that's all illusion, that no life is sacrificed, it's not possible to kill life; life only shifts form and shifts dimension; then it doesn't make any difference anymore, because you're doing a cow a favor. By eating the cow, that cow will now come into existence, you understand that. Nobody will raise cattle if nobody eats them.

Killing a human is a more sophisticated question. Killing a human, you see—the calibration of a thing depends on its intention. Intentionality. The belief that you're killing another human being and willfully defy God, and do so, then has a great karmic consequence. If you're already enlightened, you see that no such a thing is possible. First of all, you wouldn't do it because of your sense of spiritual reality. So, the question arises, is it possible on the level of the highest reality to kill another human being? What could you kill? You could kill this embodiment. "It's possible to actually kill another human being in reality—resist." (True.) "It's possible to kill their physicality—resist." (Not true.) It's possible—let's see, what do I think is the reality? "The reality is that you're volitionally forcing the person out of physicality. That's what's happening—resist." (True.) Okay. "It's not possible to kill the human being as a discrete entity—resist." (True.) It's not possible. Okay. It's not possible. You can force the person out of a physicality. Let's say the person's riding along on a horse and you shoot him, and now suddenly, the horse goes riding off with his physical body, which topples off. And the entity witnesses all this: "Oh, what right did he have to force me out of the physical body? I mean, I was still in the game, you know." So, you get knocked off the gameboard is what I see happening. My understanding is you get knocked off the chessboard, the gameboard of this time and this place in our physicality, but nothing else happens. And it was probably a karmic debt you paid off in doing that, you know.

Why doesn't the same karma apply to killing an animal? Well, you're talking about different dimensions. The belief that one is killing an animal when one kills it is why at a certain level of consciousness people are vegetarians. I was a vegetarian for 10 or 15 years. One day in a restaurant I suddenly realized what the truth of it all was, and I thought this was ridiculous. Here I am worrying about eating meat and I am meat. My physicality *is* meat. Why should I be concerned about it? So, then we shift to a different spiritual dimension in which no such thing is happening anyway, so there's nothing to worry about it.

The understanding, then, comes out of the level of consciousness out of which the question arises, not the answer. And therefore, multiple answers are possible to the same question. It's because of the intentionality of the question, the consciousness level in which it is arising, the context of it. So, there isn't like an absolute question with an absolute answer. The question and the answer constantly change, depending on how you look at it, how you contextualize it, who's asking the question at what time and in what space, and in what context. Do you understand what I'm saying? At one level, it would be, let's say, wrong to eat meat. At another, it would be wrong to not eat meat. At another level it's totally irrelevant—it doesn't arise as a question in one's mind.

* * *

Let's see. Of what importance to give the body in spiritual work? Well, the body, you would have the same reverence for the body as you would any other valuable possession, any other living thing. I try to treat my body as well as I do my kitty—not always as well as the kitty, but generally as well as the kitty. Because it's like a pet and you take good care of it. I mean, I take care of it because if I don't, I get told to.

If you haven't eaten all day, somebody says, "You haven't eaten a thing all day." I say, "Oh, all right." All these questions are significant only at certain levels, you see. To the degree to which you think your reality is your physicality would then determine how important that physicality is, washing it and putting it through purifications and various interesting things. Colonic irrigations— as I've said, the colon is not always the fastest way to God, but you go through periods of purification. People go into purification fits for years, you know. They're purifying their body of molds and fungi, and what is all that crap they don't eat? Mushrooms and candida. They imagine that there's toxins in the blood. Blood poisons. You've gotta go for a blood cleanser. Metal poisoning. There's all kinds of miasmas, night air. Used to be the night air. Used to catch tuberculosis from living in poverty neighborhoods, you know what I mean? There's all kinds of these illusions.

How much reality to give them is really answered by *A Course in Miracles*. They have as much importance as you give them. Their power of belief is what gives them any validity whatsoever. About Lesson 76 or so, it says, "I am only subject to what I hold in mind."

Right? "I am only subject to what I hold in mind." So, if you think molds will kill you, then you'd better avoid molds, because they'll kill you. So, we go through a period, though. I sort of know when people go through a period of physical concern. All kinds of cleansings, washings, purifications, and things. And then, of course, you realize you're not your physical body, and that's all sort of irrelevant. It's sort of like washing your car, and washing your car won't necessarily get you to heaven. But if you think that washing your car will get you to heaven, then the belief that it will get you to heaven will actually get you to heaven. The more often you wash your car, the higher you're going to get spiritually.

At a certain point, I think it's everybody's concern. But the idea that the blood is full of toxins and poisons and you have to take blood cleansers and blood–gastrointestinal purification. People eat all kinds of weird things—soap and powdered pumice and weird crap with chlorophyll in it—you know, to clean out your intestinal tract. If you succeed in cleaning out your intestinal tract, folks, I'm going to tell you you're going to die. Because it's only because of the bacteria that live there, the little creatures that live there and digest the food and all, that enables you to live; so, I wouldn't go cleansing out your colon too much without killing yourself. And cleansing out your blood and various things like that.

You know, I would try and lead a sort of normal life. Undue attention, undue attention to the physicality. I don't pay much attention to the thing. You do what you need to do with it. And as I say, it's sort of a toy; it's a pet. It's certainly enjoyable. I mean, if I didn't have a body I couldn't play with the kitty, could I? I couldn't cut the cake this morning. So, you know, I mean it's good for certain things, you know. But I wouldn't overemphasize the body. You know, certain meditative practices pay a great deal of attention to the body, posture, all kinds of fancy breathing exercises, visualizations, sitting on certain things and not on other things, you know. I don't think sitting on tiger skins is really cool anymore. You tell people, "Well this isn't a real tiger skin; this is a make-believe tiger skin." "Okay." And wearing lots of clothes. You know, in India, I picture people's picture of a guru is long hair and naked except for a loin cloth, sitting cross-legged on a tiger skin, right? That'll get you arrested in Sedona. It's okay to get a haircut; it's okay to take a shower; it's okay to sit on a bath towel—it doesn't have to be a tiger skin and all these things that are traditional. You see, those are not spiritual; those are ethnic. And a lot of spirituality is confused with the ethnic background out of which it arose, you know, the country of its origin, the national identities of that country, et cetera.

Spirituality is more the realization we talked about this morning, that one is the context in which content arises. There's a more advanced stage yet. There is the negation of content as self. The realization of context as self. Then, the even more advanced realization that one is both context and content, but not limited thereby. In content is the essence of context. The formless is innate within form. And that one is not just beyond form and just the formless. Nor is one just the form which one thought before one became enlightened, but one is both form and formless and therefore, one no longer separates form and formless. One is not only context but also content, that one is the formless within form. That which one is, is the formless within form, without which form could not exist, and yet, one is not limited by that form. One both "is" and "is not" at the same time because those are only categories of thought with no intrinsic reality, no self, self-substantive reality. Those are only points of observation.

Q: *"Is it appropriate or integrous to use kinesiology to help the government?"*

This is a good question. Yeah, the FBI and the CIA, right. That comes up every once in a while. Well, we did, you know a videotape, and we checked out the FBI and the CIA and the ATF. And then, the news later on revealed what we had already discovered in kinesiology. I don't know if we're allowed to do that anymore or not. In other words, the technique would have to be used integrously, and even if you, let's say, wrote Washington and say, "We used kinesiology and we found that there was a terrorist working in the Minneapolis office," they'd say, "Yeah, right." I doubt very much that it would meet with much credibility. Why is that? Because it comes out of the nonlinear, nonlinear reality, and government agencies, like science, live within linear reality. So, it sounds sort of hoo-ha to them, sort of peculiar, weird, far-out, strange. We just use it for our own information. And whenever we ask, you know, "Can we use it for the public good" or something, so far, we've always gotten no. I don't know why. It could be that the gift is a gift primarily for spiritual, for spiritual growth: "The kinesiologic method of which we are using is a gift primarily for spiritual intention—resist." (Not true.) "It's a gift for a greater than just spiritual intention—resist." (True.) "We always get a no about demonstrating it for government reasons—resist." (True.) That's true. We always get a no. I don't know why. "We don't need to know why—resist." (True.) We don't need to know. That's a break. I'm always relieved when I get that, you know, the door's shut. It says, "Don't ask about that. Thank you." Now, you're dismissed from any responsibility.

What if you're at home and you find out there's a guy named Joe and he's working in the Minneapolis office, and he's really working for the so-and-so, what's your life going to become like? Probably not too good, huh?

If you're worrying about: Shouldn't I reveal this, shouldn't I run to Washington, shouldn't I knock on doors? I mean, maybe it would not be so peaceful or good for anything or anyone. As we said, if the world as we see it is the unfoldment of a karmic coherence, if there's a karmic coherence unfolding itself, then one could be interfering with the karmic destiny of other people, agencies, entities, countries, civilizations, cultures. You know what I'm saying? You don't necessarily have that karmic entitlement to put a wrench in the monkey works. There's a nice way of putting it. So, that's a relief, folks, isn't it? We don't have to, whew, save the world.

I'd like to know any more other questions you have, because I want to make sure we complete them all. And then I want to meet with any people that want to meet with me.

* * *

The idea of treating the body as a temple is a construction, because everything is a temple, if you see it as such. Because everything is divinity coming into existence, fulfilling its potentiality.
In a discernable world of form, everything is a temple. The kitty's
kitty-ness and body is the temple of the kitty, right. Is it not? It's
God's intention of kitty-ness manifesting as kitty. "The kitty's
body is the kitty's temple—resist." (True.) Yep. So, because you see
. . . you see the divinity of all that exists; all that exists only does so
by virtue of the Creator. That which comes into existence comes
into existence as the result—as the creation by God. So, all that
exists is divine by virtue of the Source of its existence. Nothing
comes into existence except as a creation of God. Consequently,
all that exists is divine innately. The fact that it can be perceived
differently doesn't change its innate reality. A dagger is a dagger.
It is neither good nor bad. How one constructs it and perceives of
the dagger, then, makes the dagger appear to be what it is to your
intentionality and your previous programming. However, in and
of itself, the dagger is just a perfect expression of daggerness being
a dagger. Yeah, yeah. It has the capacity to come into existence. All
that exists, exists because of the divinity of its Creator.

There's a question about dealing with the esoteric. I recom-
mend generally to avoid the esoteric, the occult. In the Bible it says
to avoid the supernatural. It doesn't deny that the supernatural
exists, that there is a supernatural, that Ouija boards don't work,
that psychics are frequently correct. What it says, it doesn't say
that it's not—that it has no reality; it just says, "Don't go there."
Why don't go there? Because first of all, it's an invisible realm; you
have no idea who or what you're dealing with; what you're talking
to. You're dealing with astral realms that are full of things that
are beyond your comprehension. If you calibrate the energy field,
of various astral enterprises, entities on the other side, supposed
masters, teachers, and all these things. . . . If you calibrate the
energy level, you'll find they're usually lower astral, lower astral.
Some of them become quite famous over time, legendary almost.

But when you calibrate the energy level of that entity, it becomes apparent that your enlightenment is not what it's interested in.

First of all, you're not equipped to deal with it. You're not equipped to deal with it. Secondly, it's invisible. Unless you calibrate it, you have no idea of the level of integrity. My own experience or understanding of it is, or experience with it has been, the lower astral is filled with those energies which have denied God and hate God—refuse God. The way you get to the lower astral is you refuse, or you hate God. The only reason you do this is you're envious of God because you think that the core of your own ego is God. That refusal to give up imaginary divinity of the ego and surrender it to God is the refusal that gets you to the lower astral. The lower astral is made up of those who refuse God and hate God, but who are aware that having done so, they have now denied themselves access. The human, by virtue of the nature of being a human has the potentiality to evolve to heaven and to the presence and the awareness of God. And therefore, is hated for that. The best way to cripple the human from doing that is to ensnare him so that the most worthy prey of the lower astral is the evolving spiritual student. The spiritual student who is on their way, seriously committed and starts going into beatific spaces, swoosh—tracks them right out of the lower astral like—bang! Like gravity, they come right out like jackals waiting for the prey. What makes you vulnerable to them is your innocence. Spiritual maturity comes at considerable cost. A true teacher tries to, by advisement, give you the information you need to bypass those snares. If you get caught in the snare, the evolution of consciousness can proceed, but it can be exquisitely awful and painful and agonizing for great lengths of time.

So, the evolving spiritual aspirant . . . the naiveté is the downside in which they are attacked and get hooked. All kinds of very outlandish schemes are presented. The way to get to heaven is to kill Americans and blow them up. You know, people buy that. They buy that out of spiritual naiveté. They actually believe it. If I can convince you that going out and killing innocent people and children is serving God, then you'll do it. Hitler did it with a whole nation of people, got them to all march to their death. World War II we saw whole generations, whole nations marching off to death. And those weren't even spiritual gurus. They were just political ones. So, you see how vulnerable the human psyche is. Basically, the human psyche is innocent. It's like the hardware and you can program it with any software. Start early enough, you can program any consciousness to believe *anything*. Even when it's confronted by its opposite, it will sit there and refuse it.

I see in *Time* magazine, the Japanese spiritual leader who released the sarin gas in the Japanese subway, a very interesting follow-up article. Having gassed all these innocent people for no reason whatsoever, and not even a spiritual justification, not even rationalization, he has no lack of followers. How do you explain that? An interview with a woman there who joined that Japanese pseudo-spiritual cult *after* he did that. . . . When asked why, she said because she's afraid of death. Weird, huh? So, even somebody demonstrably demonic, even a five-year old would know that this is a demonic entity, still has no lack of followers.

So, the downside of human naiveté, then, makes us all vulnerable. If it wasn't for the fact we were all vulnerable, we all would have become Buddhas thousands of years ago. It's because we didn't know any better out of ignorance and innocence that one is prey to those who are more advanced in deception. Don't fool yourself that you are smarter than the deceptive capacity of lower astrals; you're not. The first thing that'll save you is humility. You are *not* smarter. These entities have been at it for millennia. They can sense the slightest weakness in your psyche and know just how to pull that out. And they'll have you licking their boots, thinking you're serving God. I don't want to build them up to be greater than what they are, but they are extremely clever.

So, the only thing that'll guard you against it is spiritual education and sophistication. One of the reasons that I have been a champion of the kinesiologic method is because man can't tell truth from falsehood. Unless you're intuitively quite advanced spiritually, you just don't *get* that that's out. You don't get that that's out. Sedona's full of people naively led by the nose through all kinds of astral circus stunts. By all kinds of incredulous, unbelievable entities on the other side. Sacrificing wife, children, families. You can't have sex with each other, but "you can have it with me." I mean, the delusional craziness that goes on. You say, "Nobody would believe that." Oh, yes, they do. They believe it. They believe it. In this lifetime, we've seen gurus go up and go down. We've seen them collect millions of dollars worth of vehicles, cars, millions of dollars of money, and then tell the public that they are higher than Jesus and crash. Higher than Jesus, come on. You'd have to calibrate over 1,000 to be higher than Jesus. No. So, we've seen them crash and burn, one after another. Because we're innocent, we believe in purity and goodness and all these kinds of things. We're not on our guard about such things.

One time I was in New York City in the Three Guys restaurant, and I met a well-known guru. At that time, I was enthused about a certain technique, and I said, "I think we should share this with the world. Share this with the world." See. I believe in discovering a thing and then sharing it with the world. I mean, that's what the purpose of discovering is, isn't it, to share it with the world. At this point, he became livid, livid. "Give it away for free?" I thought monasteries and the priesthood, everybody struggling with sin. And here's a way of letting go of sin as an attachment. Sin is nothing but an attachment. We'll take it to the monasteries; we'll take it to the priests; we'll take it to the public. At that point, the strangest thing happened. All of a sudden, another voice came through him. I'd known this guy for years. Another voice came through him and spoke in a totally different energy field, and it was like the door of hell opened up. A horrible energy. And it said, "Anything worth anything, if you give it away, you say that it's valueless, this and that." Then the voice went on to tell me how Jesus and the Buddha were just astrals, and how Henry Ford had done more for mankind than Jesus Christ and Buddha and all the others and Krishna and all of them together. Went on and on like that. It went on and on like that. So, it's almost like you reach a certain level of spiritual awareness, you trigger its, you might say, its opposite, you know. You want to give it away for free, instantly it wants you to sell it, you know. It's strange, you know. Totally unexpected, out of the blue.

We all know that spiritual wisdom says leave Ouija boards alone. Is that universal? We're all in agreement? You've all heard that? Has anybody told you that playing with Ouija boards is good for your spiritual awareness? Universally, it's condemned. Everybody says, "Stay away from Ouija boards." It doesn't say they don't work. It says stay away from them. It's because the astral looks to dominate you. Pretty soon, you'll be getting to want to serve the astral on the other side and the astral, he loves to gain power over a human and delay his progression to God. He says, "You're on your way as a human being. Your destiny is ultimately salvation and heaven, et cetera." The entity who has cut themself off from that potentiality gains credit in its own domain by holding you back. You understand what I'm saying? The more converts it can take out of spiritual, legitimate spiritual dimension, the greater becomes its power. Greater becomes its power. So, the rulers of great astral domains are extremely clever. Never try to pit your wits against them. They've been at it for millennia. They're experts at manipulating, dissimulating, sounding pious. All kinds of fancy names, mystery entities from ancient . . . Greek mysteries of the ancient something. "Ancient mystery"—these are called glamorizations, falsity by glamorization—"I am Master so-and-so from ancient Greece."

We know that the universe consists of the various astral domains, so-called inner planes; we know where you can go from heaven to the higher astral, to the middle astral, to the lower astral, et cetera. We know that there's heavens and hells. And we know that there's purgatories because certainly the life experience of the average human being here is purgatorial. You can go from the pits of severe pain to the highest ecstasy. You can pick the Luciferic and the satanic and the demonic, or you can pick enlightenment. So, an earthly existence is almost purgatorial in that you have a choice of all dimensions. From here you can go anywhere. And the temptations then arise from all these various dimensions. And by choice, then, your own buoyancy in the sea of choices, the karmic potentiality of evolution of consciousness, is decided from moment to moment. Every single decision changes the infinite potentiality. What purpose does it serve? I don't see that it serves any purpose. I can live without it, myself. Like a broken ankle, I mean I can get along swell without it. I think a teacher should share what he's learned about the downside, because I hear that sucking sound as people go down, and people that were once great teachers and you calibrate their early books, and now you calibrate what their consciousness level is now, or was before they died, and you saw that they crashed and burned. It would be like spiritual evolution is the enemy of that which is grossly negative. And it seeks to pull you down. It seeks to pull you down. It hates that which it sees as more powerful and more evolved than itself. That's about all I can figure out of it. Does it serve any purpose? Not any that I can see.

The seduction, the seduction of the glamourous, the pseudo-spiritually glamourous is seductive, the trappings, the gizmos that go with it. That's one reason, one of the main reasons—in fact, *the* main reason that I wrote about the levels of consciousness kinesiologic technique. I am going to think about a famous entity around Sedona right now. He's well-known. "His energy is over 200—resist." (Not true.) "The entity, his master on the other side is over 200—resist." (Not true.) Yeah. This is a guy with all kinds of followers, all kinds of crap. He talks to Master Baba on the other side, full of crap, man, I tell you, pure 100 percent BS. The naïve are sucked in by the ooh-ah-ooh. You know, the first time you get a psychic reading? It's a knockout isn't it? Somebody reads the cards, you say, "Wow, somebody reads the tarot cards." "I see your grandmother has a very advanced case of something." Wow, your grandmother does, you go, "Whew, wowsville." I mean it's a boggler, right? To the naïve, it's a boggler. It doesn't mean the astral world doesn't exist. It just means its effect on your life is going to be deleterious, because pretty soon, the entity on the other side will have control over you. You're going to want its approval; you're going to follow its advice. You're going to be investing your money in racehorses.

And, you see, you come out of a world of reason and logic, and you come into the supernatural world, everybody's knocked out about it. You know, the first time you get a psychic reading, it boggles everybody's minds the first time you get the tarot cards read. How does she know my uncle had cancer, you know what I'm saying? How'd she know that? Well, because there's more than one dimension, folks. And yet, if you hold it in mind, it's held in mind in other invisible domains as well. So, what you think is secret and unknowable except to yourself, you know, is out there. Anybody can read it. And with a little training, you yourself can read other people's psyches and there's nothing to it. So, the serious spiritual student has to abide by the cautions of the great teachers. All the great teachers have said: it isn't that it doesn't exist, and it has no reality. They say don't go there. You're not equipped to go there. You're not trained to deal with lower astrals. They can dissimulate in ways that are so convincing, that unless you're quite erudite. . . . I was in a very advanced state. I mean a very advanced state at one time beyond all form, in a state of infinite power—how would we describe the state? It stayed beyond all form, beyond all wantingness, beyond all individuality. It was at one with the infinite power of the universe. And a knowingness came on, not an entity. I've never seen any entities. A knowingness came on. The knowingness spoke thusly: "Now that you realize you're beyond individual karma, and that there is no God to which you are answerable, inasmuch as you have no karma to begin with and no such God as religion believes in even exists anyway, you're beyond all karma. You're answerable to nothing. All power is yours. Own it." That's what the knowingness came to me as. Answerable to nothing. You've got no karma to answer for, and no arbitrary God up there who's going to punish you, even if you did have karma to answer for, you don't believe in the God of the Old Testament. You're beyond form. You're beyond individual personal karma. That was true. At that point, I was totally beyond all personal karma, answerable to nothing and to no one. The power was really based on relinquishing love as any kind of reality, and seeing love as a limitation. If you let go of any kind—if you let go of love itself, then all power is yours. All power of the universe is yours. That's a fact. Same temptation that Jesus Christ was presented with. Not many people have been through that pass. It was like a very high pass. I saw who had been through there, and I saw the answer that he'd given. And the defect was to try to own the power of God, without owning the love of God. God is infinite power, also infinite love. So, the Luciferic energy tries to seal the power of God, but escape the love of God, because that would be a limitation. You can't kill off millions of people if you're still capable of love. You have to eliminate lovingness, and now you can kill them and have infinite domain over them.

Anyway, at that space the knowingness of this consciousness was already sufficiently advanced to negate that temptation and say no to it. Cannot ever be used for personal gain. I saw Jesus Christ had been there and said no to it. I saw some other gurus throughout history who had said yes to it. And I saw why they said yes. It's because they had not had the karmic gain of having been educated by their own teacher in advance to know better. So, I feel it's my responsibility to share such things, that such a thing will not befall you. Why? Because these things come unannounced, unexpected. You're just sitting there meditating or releasing on something, chanting, maybe doing the Jesus Prayer, walking through the woods, and all of a sudden it comes to you. You've got no time to think it over, how am I going to answer this, how am I going to handle it, unless you've heard about it before and can bring it right up. It'll come up. Having heard it, it comes up at the time, having heard it. You've heard it now. When that comes to you, the knowingness arises beyond thinkingness. Having heard it, one is now protected. One is now protected. So, those that have fallen, I feel a compassion for. They somehow were unprotected. Their teachers did not share with them—maybe their teachers didn't know. And so they fell over the abyss. The way back from over the abyss is hellish and can be awful and take long, long periods of time. Longer than anybody in this audience can know what I mean by "long." Long eons of time to come back from the serious fall of Grace. And so, I say this out of respect for the evolution of the consciousness of everybody in this room, because everybody in this room has reached the point of plump desirability, by that which grows stronger and stronger on your plump little innocent spirit. And so, I don't want any of my chickens eaten by them.

* * *

We are preparing a book where we're going to do a thousand calibrations, and again, it's iffy. We have to constantly ask, "Should we share this, can we share this, is this shareable, is this beneficial to the world, is it beneficial to society? Could such a thing have, you know, an unexpected negative result? So, you can't be like the bull in the China shop, you know what I'm saying? We get that the purpose is merely educational. Each of us needs to take responsibility for the evolution of our own consciousness. And in so doing, we earn a certain karmic merit. All I want people to do is to be aware, don't be naively foolish, fall for anything. Be aware that there is a downside, a certain amount of fallacy out there that masquerades as the legitimate. Jesus Christ said the same thing. He said, "Beware the wolf in sheep's clothing." He didn't know kinesiology. He didn't tell you how to differentiate them. Yes, he did. "By their fruits, ye shall know them." Okay, so all we've had to go, as far as discernment, spiritual discernment over the ages has been, "By their fruits we shall know them." We could say killing three thousand innocent people would indicate that this is probably not of the most pure and delicate, you know. "By their fruits we shall know them." So, that's all we've had to go by and, by karmic merit apparently in the late 1980s, we were likely given a way of telling the wolf from the sheep. We never had one before. And of course, the desire to write the book *Power vs. Force* came from the excitement of discovering, my God, we've got a way of telling wolf in the sheep's clothing from the sheep from the wolf, for the first time. And as I've said, I spent some years agonizing over how to share it and whether I should share it, and in what style and how to best present it and to give it the most possible respect. I went through all the work of getting a Ph.D. and putting it through routine scientific presentation as "Quantitative and Qualitative Analysis and Calibrations of Levels of Human Consciousness" through a university faculty, and I had all the statistics done by a statistical firm that ran it through all their computers, et cetera. So, I made sure first that it was solid on a scientific, rational, logical basis because from that we were going to then move through levels of consciousness, from the linear Newtonian domain to the nonlinear spiritual domain, the reality of which was already apparent to me, having totally experienced it, at age 37.

When it came on, the totality of the absoluteness of the presence of God was so stunning and profound that it staggered me out for 10 years, and I never did mention it for 30 years, in fact—never did mention it. So, I think we're safe if we respect that we owe it to the divinity within us. I say, "I owe it to God to share what I have learned." I owe it to God to share what I have learned with others for whatever benefit. I have to share whatever benefit I have gained with them. That mankind will not be led down the dark path to hell the way he has in the past because he certainly has been seduced into hell in the past, has he not? The great seducers of mankind are historically—and many of them still celebrated.

So that is where we'll conclude. I've tried to share all that I can that I feel would be most beneficial and helpful and to be guarded on your way. To have the "breastplate of truth," as Jesus said. Isn't that what he said, the "breastplate of truth"? To guard one against what I call "spiritual seductions." Spiritual seduction, and to be aware that there are those entities within the universe who do not have your enlightenment as their interest. They are not interested in your salvation or your enlightenment. In fact, they gain their power, prestige, and domains by destroying yours.

CONCLUSION

We anticipate that by reading this volume you will have a greater understanding of the spiritual concepts Dr. Hawkins conveyed with his lighthearted spirit yet in-depth manner. Through self-honesty, contemplation, and a willingness to see the truth, deeper insights can happen bringing you inner peace, compassion, and the subjective experience of living from a higher field of consciousness.

Read this book often or watch or listen to the May and June 2002 lectures that are available. One never knows when that aha moment will occur, but through continual repetition of the material, as Dr. Hawkins has counseled, the likelihood that it will transpire is higher.

The following points are some of the inspiring truths in this book that you can contemplate as you go through your day:

- All truth is only true within a certain context. The Infinite context is what spirituality is all about.

- For anything to be what it is at this moment, it must fulfill the potentiality, which is innate to its existence.

- "What you hold in mind tends to manifest." It tends to manifest because you're influencing the infinite quantum potentiality.

- That which is of God brings peace and love.

167

- Divinity is the source of your own existence. It is out of divinity that consciousness arises.

- The condition of loving prevails as a permanency because it's what you are. It's what you have become.

- All spiritual work is in essence, renunciation. You're renouncing the negative for the positive.

- Renunciation in its essence, is the essence of all spiritual work, because you're at all times renouncing it (the negative) as an attachment, renouncing it as a value, renouncing it as a way that you choose to go. So, by choosing the positive, you're always renouncing the negative. To renounce allowing a certain thing to dominate your consciousness.

- Free will comes in, then, in choosing to go in the direction of God. The choice to go in the direction of spiritual truth as one understands it at this point of the evolution of one's own consciousness.

- At its highest level, a meditation is merely the manner in which you contextualize your experience of aliveness.

Dr. Hawkins states: ". . . We all serve all of life through all of our spiritual endeavors. Everything that we surrender to God, for the good of all, every advance, every forgiveness that we personally do, every time we let go of feeling sad and unhappy, and every negativity we let go, benefits all of mankind. Consequently, anybody who is in spiritual endeavor is of service to man at all times, just by their intention." (May 2002 lecture)

Straight and Narrow Is the Path . . . Waste No Time.
Gloria in Excelsis Deo!

APPENDIX

PROGRESSIVE FIELDS OF REALIZATION

Form

Register

Recognition

Watcher/Experiencer

Awareness

Observer/Witness

Light of Consciousness

Manifest as Allness/Self

Unmanifest (Godhead)

Slide 22

Newtonian Paradigm vs. Quantum Mechanics

Newtonian Paradigm	Quantum Mechanics
Orderly	Disorderly
Logical	Illogical
Predictable	Unpredictable
Deterministic	Free
Literal	Creative
Pedestrian	Imaginative
Reductionist	Progressive
Separate	Intermingled, Interconnected
Discrete	Diffuse
Cause	Potentiate
Atomistic	Nonlocal Coherence
Forced	Reactive
Caused	Responsive
Provable	Comprehensible
Measurable	Observable
Sequential	Simultaneous
Settled	Potential
Temporal	Time Dependent/Independent
Computational	Stochastic/Chaotic
Limited	Unlimited
Actuality	Possibility
Permanent	Altered by Observation
Constricted	Expansive
Content	Context
Objective	Subjective
Force	Power
Certain	Uncertain
Finished	Poised

ABOUT THE AUTHOR

David R. Hawkins, M.D., Ph.D. (1927–2012), was director of the Institute for Spiritual Research, Inc., and founder of the Path of Devotional Nonduality. He was renowned as a pioneering researcher in the field of consciousness as well as an author, lecturer, clinician, physician, and scientist. He served as an advisor to Catholic and Protestant churches, and Buddhist monasteries; appeared on major network television and radio programs; and le ctured widely at such places as Westminster Abbey, the Oxford Forum, the University of Notre Dame, and Harvard University. His life was devoted to the upliftment of mankind until his death in 2012.

For more information on Dr. Hawkins's work, visit **veritaspub.com**.

Notes

Notes

Notes

Notes

Notes

Notes

Hay House Titles of Related Interest

YOU CAN HEAL YOUR LIFE, the movie,
starring Louise Hay & Friends
(available as an online streaming video)
www.hayhouse.com/louise-movie

THE SHIFT, the movie,
starring Dr. Wayne W. Dyer
(available as an online streaming video)
www.hayhouse.com/the-shift-movie

***

*THE BIOLOGY OF BELIEF: Unleashing the Power of Consciousness,
Matter & Miracles* by Bruce H. Lipton, Ph.D.

*DIRECTING OUR INNER LIGHT: Using Meditation to
Heal the Body, Mind, and Spirit* by Brian L. Weiss, M.D.

*INTENTIONALITY: A Groundbreaking Guide to Breath, Consciousness,
and Radical Self-Transformation* by Finnian Kelly

*PURE HUMAN: The Hidden Truth of Our Divinity, Power,
and Destiny* by Gregg Braden

All of the above are available at your local bookstore,
or may be ordered by contacting Hay House (see next page).

***

We hope you enjoyed this Hay House book. If you'd like to receive our online catalog featuring additional information on Hay House books and products, or if you'd like to find out more about the Hay Foundation, please contact:

Hay House LLC, P.O. Box 5100, Carlsbad, CA 92018-5100
(760) 431-7695 or (800) 654-5126
www.hayhouse.com® • www.hayfoundation.org

———

Published in Australia by:
Hay House Australia Publishing Pty Ltd
18/36 Ralph St., Alexandria NSW 2015
Phone: +61 (02) 9669 4299
www.hayhouse.com.au

Published in the United Kingdom by:
Hay House UK Ltd
1st Floor, Crawford Corner,
91–93 Baker Street, London W1U 6QQ
Phone: +44 (0)20 3927 7290
www.hayhouse.co.uk

Published in India by:
Hay House Publishers (India) Pvt Ltd
Muskaan Complex, Plot No. 3,
B-2, Vasant Kunj, New Delhi 110 070
Phone: +91 11 41761620
www.hayhouse.co.in

———

Let Your Soul Grow

Experience life-changing transformation—one video
at a time—with guidance from the world's leading experts.

www.healyourlifeplus.com